Contents

Acknowledgments

We would like to thank the staff of young carers projects and carers centres for their cooperation and support in this research. We are also grateful to the project advisory group, Penny Banks, Paul Field, Charlie Lloyd, Imelda Redmond, Bill Riddell, Janine Shaw and Michele Wates for their helpful comments on an earlier draft of the report and their support throughout the life of the project. Our thanks also go to the Joseph Rowntree Foundation for funding the research. Finally and most importantly, we would like to thank all the young people who gave up their time to be interviewed and who shared with us what were sometimes difficult and painful experiences. Without them this research would not have been possible.

Chris Dearden and Saul Becker

Summary

The study

This is a study of 60 young people who are either caring now, or have cared at some time in the past, for a parent with an illness or disability. The study examines young carers' transitions to adulthood and identifies the factors associated with caring that affect such transitions.

The policy background to the study is one of tensions, contradictions and ambiguities. Community care policy assumes that family members will provide much of the care and support required by relatives, with the state stepping in to fill the gaps. However, childhood is viewed as a distinct phase and one that is protected. While adults are therefore expected to adopt 'caring' roles, children transgress social norms if they do so. However, younger, disabled or ill adults who have dependent children may often lack the necessary social care provision or financial resources, which can result in their children sometimes adopting inappropriate caring roles. While this has been recognised in recent years and specialist support to young carers has been developed in some parts of the country, services that support disabled adults as parents have not developed as rapidly or as extensively.

Other policies have had an impact on young people. The collapse of the youth labour market, the introduction of training schemes for young people and vocationalism within education have delayed young people's transitions to adulthood. At the same time, changes to the benefit system have removed eligibility for most 16 and 17-year-olds and reduced benefit payments to under 25s. The erosion of student grants and the introduction of loans and tuition fees have increased young people's financial dependence on their families. Such policies, as the study confirms, result in some families relying on their children to provide support in the absence of appropriate alternatives, and in children relying on families to support them financially, even though illness and disability are strongly associated with poverty and social exclusion for all family members.

There are several factors that influence whether young caring occurs within families. The most critical one is the receipt of external support services that take into account and meet the needs of the whole family.

Profile of the respondents

- 60 young carers were interviewed in depth about their experiences and transitions – 36 respondents were aged 16 to18; 24 aged 19 to 25.
- Most were women; 24 in the younger age group, 21 in the older group.
- Only four were from minority ethnic communities.
- Half were living in lone parent families.
- One-third of parents were owner-occupiers; most were in rented accommodation.
- None of the parents who were ill or disabled were in employment; most had been in manual occupations.
- In two-parent families about a third of the second parents were in employment, most in manual occupations.
- Two-thirds of respondents were caring for mothers; seven were caring for more than one person.
- Two-thirds of parents had physical health problems; one-third had mental health problems.

- Most young people were performing domestic tasks; over half were providing general care; almost half were providing personal care; one-third were offering emotional support; a few were caring for younger siblings in addition to one or more caring responsibilities.

Education, training and employment

- A large proportion of young carers had educational problems and missed school. Many failed to attain any educational qualifications.
- Education welfare and teaching staff often colluded in young carers' absence from school.
- A lack of educational qualifications combined with ongoing caring responsibilities served to exclude some young carers from the labour market.
- In the absence of education maintenance allowances and labour market opportunities, continuing to care appeared understandable in some families.

Cash and care: income, benefits and services

- Virtually all the families were in receipt of welfare benefits and were outside the paid labour market. Experience of poverty and social exclusion was common.
- While some families did receive helpful and valued services, one-third received nothing at all and some had cancelled services that they viewed as intrusive, unnecessary, poor quality or too expensive.
- Once young caring became established families

were more likely to cancel services.
- Where families received good quality and reliable support and services this reduced young people's caring roles.
- There was no evidence of any services specifically to support disabled parents in their parenting role.

Leaving home: permanent and temporary transitions

- Leaving home was especially problematic for many young carers, particularly if they had to leave a parent who required considerable help and support. Some young people delayed this transition to spatial independence.
- In families where a parent had a severe and enduring mental health problem, young carers' spatial transitions were sometimes premature and traumatic if, for example, the young person reached crisis point or had to be received into public care.

Becoming an adult: young people's perspectives

- The positive impacts of caring included maturity, responsibility and life skills and a close and loving relationship with parents. The negative impacts included stress and depression, restricted social, educational and career opportunities, and less time for oneself.
- Young people's choices were both influenced and restricted by caring. Some young people left home either earlier or later than they would have chosen. Career and job choice were

sometimes influenced by the skills gained through caring, but restricted by the lack of formal qualifications.

- Maturity, responsibility, decision-making and the acquisition of practical skills were viewed as important and useful for independence and adulthood and were often gained through caring. However, opportunity and other personal costs accompanied the acquisition of these skills.

Implications for policy and practice

- Many families received no or inadequate social care services. Where services were provided they were sometimes inappropriate, intrusive or too costly. Early interventions may prevent inappropriate caring roles from becoming established.
- Services that support disabled adults in their parenting role are rare. Their needs are rarely *specifically* mentioned in local authority plans.
- Professionals from all sectors need more understanding of the social model of disability.
- Social services, health, education and the voluntary sector all have a responsibility to prevent young caring from occurring by early recognition and positive interventions which focus on the needs of the whole family.
- Assessments must recognise the needs and rights of both parents and children. Services must meet these needs and rights.
- Schools can compound young carers' educational difficulties and disadvantages by not entering them for public examinations or by failing to recognise their specific educational, social and developmental needs.

- Those young carers who have negative educational experiences or outcomes should be offered a 'second chance'.
- Where young carers do miss school, there needs to be a better, more even balance between punitive interventions (such as threats of court action) and collusion (by condoning unauthorised absences).
- In some circumstances, particularly where a parent has a terminal illness, this balanced approach should meet the wishes of the child to spend time with their parent.
- Many young carers often have key skills and competencies that go unrecognised and there is currently no way of accrediting such skills. While the acquisition of such skills will not be best achieved by caring unsupported, such skills, if acknowledged, would be an asset to many employers.
- Careers advisers need to be aware of these skills and competencies and try to offer a range of possible options rather than allowing young people to limit their choices to 'caring' jobs.
- The widespread absence of education maintenance allowances and grants for those in further and higher education discriminates against poorer families and those where young people are unable to take part-time work because of caring commitments.
- There is a need to recognise and respond to the specific needs of young adult carers aged 18 to 25 who do not seem to make use of (adult) carer support facilities while being too old to access most young carer provision.
- Some children and young people may choose to become carers for their parents. In such cases they should have the right to services and benefits which will assist them in their role as carers.

- The benefit system does not recognise the particular needs of ill or disabled parents who have adolescent children. Poverty, illness, lone parenthood and lack of support may make supporting older children more difficult.

- The lack of available single-person housing and age discrimination in relation to tenancies and leases can cause problems for 'early leavers' who are, or feel, unable to remain in the parental home.

- Employment and education policies in particular need to be better coordinated to recognise young carers' specific needs and the 'Catch 22' situations that many of them face.

- Health care professionals have a responsibility to ensure that adequate support and services are in place following illness or disability. More liaison between health and social care professionals and better provision and coordination of services will reduce families' reliance on children.

- While health care professionals have a duty and responsibility to provide families with information and advice, this should not extend to training children to perform inappropriate caring tasks.

- Currently some areas of the country have young carers projects while others do not. Disabled adults have little support as parents. Supporting either parent or child in isolation is not sufficient; support for whole families is essential. Young carers' independence cannot be separated from their parent's independence. It is not possible to have true independence for one without independence for the other. The emphasis in policy and practice should be on preventing children from taking on inappropriate caring responsibilities in the first place, and stopping these roles from becoming institutionalised where and when they have already begun. Policies and services which identify and respond to the needs of all family members, but in particular those which support ill or disabled parents to enable them to prevent inappropriate caring roles from developing, will offer the best way forward. This challenges us all to think critically about how services to ill and disabled parents, and to existing young carers, should be structured, what they should do, and how they should fit together. Such a rethink would mean fundamental change to the existing structures for young carers' services, and the emergence of new and empowering services for ill and disabled parents. Are we up to the challenge?

1 Introduction

In this chapter we will offer a definition of young caring and give four brief profiles of respondents. These cases have been chosen to demonstrate to the reader a range of young carers' experiences, including parental physical and mental health problems, the receipt or non-receipt of external services, experience of local authority care, and post-school experiences. There is no 'typical' young carer, all are individual and have unique experiences. However, these profiles give the reader a greater insight into the lives of four of the respondents.

We will then place young caring in a research, policy and practice context, outlining the research background to the study and identifying key legislation and policy and practice initiatives. Finally, we will briefly describe the methodology adopted.

Defining our terms

Young carers are children and young people who provide care or support to a relative in the home. They provide similar levels of support to adult carers but their experiences differ because those under the age of 18 are legally defined as *children* and, as such, are not expected to take on significant or substantial caring roles. However, community care policy and legislation assume that family members will provide the bulk of care in the community with the state stepping in to fill the gaps[1]. In some families this results in children and young people adopting caring roles, often, although not exclusively, in the absence of another adult in the home. While adult carers can therefore be seen to be conforming to societal norms in supporting family members, when children act as carers they transgress such norms. In theory at least, childhood is viewed as a protected phase, with adults, and the state, supporting and protecting children and young people until they make the transition into adulthood. Not all children with ill or disabled parents will become young carers. One may assume that in families with adequate support, services and finances, most children will not be adversely affected. *The Blackwell Encyclopaedia of Social Work* defines young carers as:

'Children and young persons under 18 who provide or intend to provide care, assistance or support to another family member. They carry out, often on a regular basis, significant or substantial caring tasks and assume a level of responsibility which would usually be associated with an adult.

'The person receiving care is often a parent but can be a sibling, grandparent or other relative who is disabled, has some chronic illness, mental health problem or other condition connected with a need for care, support or supervision.

'Factors which influence the extent and nature of young carers' tasks and responsibilities include the illness/disability, family structure, gender, culture, religion, income, and the availability and quality of professional support and services.

'Where children and families lack appropriate professional support and adequate income then some young carers experience impaired psycho-social development, including poor educational attendance and performance, and restricted peer networks, friendships and opportunities. These will have implications for their own adulthood. Young carers have rights to an assessment and support under legislation. Specialist projects are one way of meeting their needs.'[2]

This study aims to identify these implications by looking at young carers' transitions from childhood to adulthood.

Profiles of four respondents

Case 1

Graham is 16 and lives with his mother and 13-year-old sister. His parents separated about three years ago and he has no contact with his father. The family lives in council accommodation and his mother receives child benefit, income support and possibly another benefit. Graham's mother has Myasthenia Gravis (a disease that affects the muscles and results in extreme tiredness and weakness) and diabetes. She may also have cancer. She is very weak and cannot walk very far. She was told 12 years ago that she would probably not live beyond 10 years.

Graham empties his mother's commode, collects her benefit, helps with the housework, does most of the cooking, lifts his mother out of her chair and in and out of the bath when she is feeling very weak and sometimes washes her hair. He also helps her to monitor her blood sugar. The level of care that Graham provides has increased as his mother's condition has deteriorated and he has also done more since his father left.

Graham and his sister receive support from a young carers project but his mother has no outside services. Graham doesn't know whether services have ever been offered but said he would not want a stranger coming into the home and taking over tasks that he already does.

Graham is currently in further education doing plastering having left school at 16. He cannot remember his GCSE results but didn't have any A–C passes. He has no independent income although his mother gives him money when she can afford to. She is currently in rent arrears and there is very little money available to them.

Case 2

Sharon is 17 and lives with her father and 12-year-old brother. Her parents separated about 12 years ago and she has contact with her mother several times a year. The family live in council accommodation and her father receives child benefit and disability living allowance. Sharon's father has had back problems, mental health problems and alcohol problems for about 10 years. More recently he has had a heart attack.

Both Sharon and her brother have been in foster care when their father's alcohol and mental health problems were severe. During the longest period they were in care (just under a year) they were separated from each other and sent to different carers.

Sharon does most of the housework and shopping and she and her father share the cooking. She has done these tasks since she was about 13, gradually taking on more responsibility as she has got older. She is hoping that her brother will do more as he gets older. She finds the uncertainty of her father's alcohol and mental health problems stressful.

Sharon's father has a 'befriender', arranged by social services and a very supportive GP. Sharon and her brother receive support from a young carers project. The family has no practical help.

Sharon left school at 16 and took GCSEs, achieving grades D–F in all subjects. She is currently in further education doing a social care course, which she feels was influenced by her experiences at home. She has no independent income but receives some money from her father.

Case 3

Mike is 19 and lives with his mother. He has three older siblings who all left home several years ago. His parents divorced when he was about 8 or 9 and he has had no contact with his father for over four years. His mother has since remarried and divorced. Mike's mother owns her own home and receives disability living allowance. She has a degenerative spinal problem that sometimes causes severe pain. She finds it difficult to walk, using crutches indoors and a wheelchair outside. Although the condition has been present for a long time, it has been worse over the past six or seven years (since Mike was about 11 or 12).

Mike gradually started to take on domestic tasks from the age of 13. Two years ago, when his mother's second marriage had ended he also began to provide more personal care. At this point a care package reduced the level of practical, domestic support he provided. More recently, following a hospital admission, his mother's care package has been increased and she now has carers three times a day, removing the need for Mike to provide personal care.

Mike left school at 16 having attained nine GCSE passes at grades A–C. He then did A-levels at college and is now working part-time before going to university.

Case 4

Karen is 22 and lives with her parents and older brother. She has an older sister who has left home. Her parents own their home. Her father works full-time in a manual occupation and her mother, who has rheumatoid arthritis, receives disability living allowance. Karen's grandparents live close by and her grandmother has had a stroke, which has left her requiring total nursing care.

Karen's mother has been ill since Karen was 12. Initially Karen took on domestic chores such as housework, cooking, etc. At that point her grandmother helped her. She also provided personal care to her mother, helping her to wash and dress. Over a period of four years Karen provided personal and practical care but her caring responsibilities slightly reduced from the age of 16 as her mother's condition began to improve. When Karen was 18 her grandmother suffered a severe stroke. Karen was still providing care for her mother and took on a caring role for her grandmother as well. She now receives invalid care allowance and is classed as her mother's full-time carer although in addition she actually provides a high level of practical and personal care for her grandmother and emotional support to her grandfather. Karen's mother receives some support from a voluntary care attendant scheme and her grandmother has home care twice daily and three nights a week.

Karen left school at 16. Her mother was in hospital when she did her GCSEs and she feels this is why she only achieved A–C passes in three subjects. She then did a BTEC course at college and planned to go to university before her grandmother became ill. She is now a full-time carer and has never entered the labour market.

The context of the study: research, policy and practice

Since the mid-1980s there has been an increased awareness of the existence of children and young people as carers. Early research sought to establish the extent of the 'problem'[3] and, while failing in its attempts to indicate potential numbers of young carers, stimulated further research into the needs and experiences of such children and young people. Early small-scale qualitative studies, such as those by Bilsborrow[4] and Aldridge and Becker[5] identified the experiences of young carers, often drawing on their own words. Aldridge and Becker[6] also conducted the first study of parents with an illness or disability who were supported by their children. Other studies have sought to ascertain the experiences of, or effects on, children in families where a parent has a specific illness or disability, such as Parkinson's Disease[7], mental health problems[8], multiple sclerosis[9] and HIV/AIDS[10].

As awareness of young carers' issues has grown and support for them has increased it has become easier to identify them in larger numbers and to conduct more detailed quantitative studies. By contacting specialist support services it is now possible to generate statistical information about larger numbers of young carers. In 1995 the first such survey was conducted[11] and information was collated on 640 young people supported by specialist young carers' projects. This survey was replicated in 1997 and generated data on more than 2,300 young carers, including information relating to social services' assessments of young carers[12]. These two national surveys provide a background to this piece of research.

Alongside the growing body of research into young caring has come increased professional awareness and support for young carers. In 1992 the first two pilot projects to support young carers were established. By 1995 there were 37 such projects and in 2000 over 115. The majority of specialist support projects are located within the voluntary sector but most receive some form of statutory funding. Official documents increasingly recognise the particular needs of young carers[13], and the Department of Health has issued guidance to all local authority social services departments regarding their duties to young carers. Furthermore, the Department of Health undertook its own programme of work relating to young carers[14] and

sought to establish an estimate of the number of young carers nationally[15]. While this figure – somewhere between 19,000 and 50,000 – is somewhat crude, being based on a small subsample of the population, it does indicate that government departments are taking the issue seriously. However, this 'official' figure is based on the definition of carers used in the 1995 Carers Act, namely those people who provide, or intend to provide, *substantial care on a regular basis*. As such it fails to encompass all children and young people who may not provide substantial or regular care but whose lives (and childhood) may be adversely affected by their caring roles and responsibilities. *The Blackwell Encyclopaedia*[16] definition, cited previously, is broader than the 'official' one.

While awareness, research and policy relating to young carers have developed there has been little development in policy or practice regarding disabled parents. This skewed development has meant that while support for young carers has increased, some local authorities feel that the 'problem' has been solved and have done little to support ill and disabled parents in their parenting roles. This has led some commentators to suggest that highlighting the experiences of young carers serves to undermine disabled parents[17] and that providing services to young carers deflects attention and scarce resources away from their disabled parents[18]. There has also been some confusion in support for young carers, resulting in a lack of clarity about what specialist support services should be providing or doing. Some of the better organised and managed young carers' projects assist whole families in accessing the support services to which they are entitled, and try to ameliorate some of the more negative outcomes associated with young caring in families which do not have adequate support or services. However, others have concentrated on giving children and young people a 'good time', providing leisure activities for young carers while doing little to support whole families and to prevent these negative outcomes.

There are also many tensions and contradictions in policy and legislation relating to community care and to young people. For example, community care policy rests on the assumption that family members are the best people to provide care and support to their relatives in the community, but does not specifically take into account the needs and wishes of disabled parents who require support. The changes in policy relating to youth employment and access to benefits for young people, discussed in more detail in Chapter 3, assume that families will financially support young people for increasing lengths of time. Again, these policies do not take into account the specific experiences of families where illness or disability reduces family incomes and increases care needs. These factors may make it very difficult for some families to provide financial support to their teenage children. The 1995 Carers (Recognition and Services) Act gives all carers, including young carers, the right to request an assessment of their own needs as carers. The Carers and Disabled Children's Services Bill, going through Parliament in early 2000, makes provision for carers to receive direct payments in their own right. While these policies recognise the needs of existing young carers, they may 'institutionalise' young caring, resulting in an assumption that it is acceptable for children to continue to provide care and support providing they receive appropriate recognition. The Quality Protects initiative is intended to ensure that the children of parents with disability or specific health needs enjoy the same life chances as other children[19]. However, this is unlikely to happen

unless disabled adults are supported as parents. Policy in respect of disabled parents, as we have seen, has not advanced at the same rate as policy in respect of young carers. Current policy and practice initiatives are therefore failing to prevent young caring from starting in the first place.

Where young caring has become established, young carers can be classed as children in need, as defined by section 17 of the 1989 Children Act. However, few young carers receive assessments under the Children Act and of those who do, we have no way currently of knowing whether they are assessed as children in need or children at risk[20]. Recent policy has improved the assessment procedure for children in need to incorporate three domains: the child's developmental needs, parenting capacity, and family and environmental factors[21]. Future assessments should therefore take into account the needs of young carers, the needs and capacities of their disabled parents and environmental factors such as poverty, housing, etc. This should result in better assessments of existing young carers and support for the wider family.

The research already conducted into young caring provides us with a detailed picture of young people around the UK who have been recognised and identified as carers and who have received support from specialist carers' and young carers' centres and groups. We will draw on the major findings of previous research and surveys throughout this report. Although we still know very little about those young people *not* identified and supported as young carers, as social services departments and the voluntary sector become aware of and engage with young carers' issues, their experiences and needs have been found to be broadly similar across the country.

However, while we are aware of how caring

affects young people still classified and protected as children, we have little knowledge of whether providing significant or substantial care or support to a parent influences young people's transitions into adulthood.

'Transition to adulthood is the process by which young people move away from dependence for primary, emotional and financial support from their childhood family or carers. They enter a new era of employment or training and their needs for income, shelter and social life are met from a wider range of sources, directed by their own choice and control instead of by their parents or carers. Of course, family and childhood friends and links remain important for most young people as they move into adult life, but it is a healthy and normal process that they should seek to be in control of their own lives and to have relationships outside the family which may become important in establishing the course of their future.'[22]

The aim of this research is to establish if, and in what ways, caring might influence young people's transitions into adulthood and to identify policies which might prevent young caring from occurring, or prevent families from suffering the adverse consequences of the social effects of disability.

Methodology

The methodology adopted was semi-structured interviews with 60 young people who are either currently caring or have cared in the past for a parent or carer. The young people fall into two different age bands. Thirty-six young people were aged 16 to 18 years. This can be considered the first phase of young adulthood, as between these ages

young people achieve many cultural and legal milestones. They can buy cigarettes at 16; have heterosexual relations at 16 and male homosexual ones at 18; they complete compulsory education at 16 and make decisions relating to further education, training or employment; they may marry or leave home at 16 with parental permission; at 18 they achieve majority and are no longer classified (or protected) as children. Parents relinquish 'parental responsibility' for their children (as defined by the 1989 Children Act) once they reach 18.

Our second group of respondents, 24 young people in total, were between the ages of 19 and 25 – a period which may be classified as the second phase of transition. Although majority is achieved at 18, young people under 25 continue to be treated differently within the law. The legal minimum wage (which was introduced during the course of the research) treats young people differently, assuming that a full wage is not required by younger adults. Equally the social security system treats young people under 25 as 'semi-adults', requiring a lower level of benefits. Between the ages of 19 and 25 many young people may be forming relationships, leaving the parental home and possibly embarking on parenthood themselves.

Recruiting respondents

All of the young people who agreed to take part in the research were contacted via support services for carers. Once again this excludes those young people not already identified and supported by professionals. A further reason for identifying respondents via existing services is the hidden nature of caring, particularly when undertaken by children and young people. Using specialist support services to recruit respondents saves time and money and makes identification more straightforward.

All of the young carers' projects in the UK were contacted and asked to forward letters on our behalf to any young people between the ages of 16 and 25 with whom they were in contact. Over 500 letters were forwarded. The letters contained a brief questionnaire designed to assess whether the young people met the research criteria and whether they were willing to take part in the research. By contacting young people in this way, only those who were willing to take part returned the questionnaire and project staff were not obliged to breach confidentiality by passing on personal details to us.

The process of recruitment was very time-consuming and even with the assistance of project staff it was difficult to identify young people from the older age groups. The final sample was predominantly young women – 24 out of 36 in the 16 to 18 group and 21 out of 24 in the 19 to 25 group. We know from previous surveys[23] that a slightly higher proportion of young carers supported by projects are female and, as they get older, the gender imbalance becomes greater. Secondary analysis of the 1997 national survey indicates that in the 16 to 18 age group 66 per cent were female.

The respondents were almost exclusively white European, with only four in total from minority ethnic communities. Support for young carers from minority ethnic communities has been slow to develop and only 14 per cent of young people supported by projects in 1997 were from such communities although some individual projects support a high proportion of minority ethnic young carers. Recent research[24] indicates that young carers from South Asian communities have broadly similar needs to their white counterparts but that they face the additional problem of racism and that services which purport to be 'culturally sensitive' can sometimes end up relying on cultural stereotypes,

effectively neglecting Asian young carers' needs. The small number of minority ethnic carers in this study precludes us from drawing any specific conclusions regarding their transitions into adulthood.

There are several possible explanations for the difficulties we experienced in recruiting respondents from the older age group. First, many of the support services for young carers have an upper age limit of 18. This is usually because they are funded as children's services and, as such, are unable to support adults, i.e. those over the age of 18. Second, even where projects do support older young carers, their need for organised leisure activities (provided by many of the projects) and one-to-one support in a child-centred environment appear to diminish as they get older. Third, the difficulties in contacting carers from the 19 to 25 age group either via services for young (i.e. child) or adult carers lead us to believe that this is a group which may lack specific support, falling between the gap of children's and adult support services. Indeed, few of the older respondents were actively involved with or receiving support from carers projects. Some had remained in contact with staff from projects and had therefore been informed of the research, others remained on record as previous clients and had therefore been forwarded letters.

The interview process

The interviews were semi-structured, intended to cover a range of themes and issues considered important in the transition from childhood to adulthood. These themes included family structure and the nature of illness/disability; education, training and employment; income and benefits; receipt of and experiences of services; housing, leaving home and family separations; and becoming an adult. While all of the interviews touched on these themes, the respondents themselves led us and this enabled them to raise and discuss other issues that were clearly important to them. This type of loosely structured interview or 'conversation with a purpose'[25] has been particularly useful in eliciting information of a personal and sometimes painful nature in our previous research with young carers. Thus, not all of the interviews covered the same areas in the same order and some included information missing from others. The resulting data are both rich and detailed and include information and accounts important to the respondents as well as the researchers. The voices of the young people remain paramount, allowing us to elicit their views relating to growing up and moving into adulthood while providing support to an ill or disabled parent.

The interviews were conducted face-to-face with two exceptions where logistical difficulties resulted in telephone interviews. The majority of respondents were alone during interviews although one had a friend present and another a partner. Each interview lasted between 45 minutes and two hours, with most taking approximately 60 to 90 minutes. While the majority of interviews took place in respondents' homes, some were conducted in support projects and others in public places such as cafes – venues chosen by the young people themselves.

All interviews were recorded and fully transcribed. They were then analysed using a grounded theory approach[26], allowing the young people's own words to form the building blocks to our own understanding of their situations. Throughout the report we draw on their words to gain an understanding of their experiences as they have grown and matured from children, making the transition, sometimes partial and sometimes complete, to adulthood.

In the next chapter we take a more detailed look at the respondents and their situations.

2 The respondents

In total 60 interviews were conducted, 36 in the 16 to 18 age group and 24 in the 19 to 25 age group. The sample included four pairs of siblings. While the basic criterion for inclusion in the research was caring for a parent, either now or at some time in the past, the sample includes one young woman who was caring for her grandparents, one of whom had died. She was included because, following her parents' divorce, her grandparents became her main carers while her father was at work. When they became ill, therefore, she took responsibility for providing care and support to them, moving into their home to do so.

Some of the respondents were no longer providing support to their parents. Three parents had died and another three had gone into residential care. In these cases the young people were able to reflect on the entire process of caring, from beginning to end (although those with parents in residential care continued to have regular contact with them and offered support when necessary). In some cases either the young person or the parent had left the family home and the level of support had, in some instances, decreased.

In this section we give a more detailed breakdown of the respondents in relation to gender; ethnicity; family structure; socio-economic status; caring relationships; the nature of the illness or disability of care recipients; and caring tasks. While, where appropriate, we shall do this for each of the two age categories, it should be noted that age is only one, and not necessarily the most important, variable. It will become apparent throughout the report that other factors such as the nature of parental illness or disability, family structure, family income and the receipt of services are equally, and in some instances more important variables in determining outcomes of caring and transitions into adulthood.

Since the sample size is comparatively small and intended to be illustrative rather than representative we have avoided the widespread use of statistics. We have, however, given proportions or numbers where appropriate to give the reader an idea of the frequency of certain events occurring. This is the case throughout the report.

Gender and ethnicity

The majority of respondents were white and female. Two-thirds of the younger age group and almost all of the older were women and only four in total came from minority ethnic backgrounds.

Family structure

Half of both age groups were living in lone parent families at the time caring took place. In one case (two siblings) the parent requiring support, a father with mental health problems, left the family home and the level of support has now decreased. In other cases the parents had been together at the onset of illness but had since separated, a situation not uncommon and highlighted in other research. Family structure is a significant variable since, in lone parent families where a parent becomes ill or disabled and requires some level of care or support, there is usually no other adult available within the home to adopt that role. This does not mean that the presence of a second adult necessarily precludes children and young people from providing care and support.

Socio-economic status

Research into young caring has rarely addressed socio-economic status, focusing instead on young people's experiences and roles. Since the children and young people have always been the focus of the research (with the exception of Aldridge and Becker's[27] small-scale study of parents being supported by their children) little information has been gleaned about their parents other than the nature of their illnesses and the level of support they receive or require. However, research has shown that poverty is a key variable in determining outcomes for children who care and for their ill or disabled parents[28].

In this study we isolated two factors which give an indication of socio-economic status – housing and parental employment status. While these factors are fairly crude measures, it was not possible to establish income levels (a more reliable measure) since we did not speak directly to parents. We did, however, look at the incidence of benefit receipt, which is discussed in more detail in Chapter 4.

Overall, the majority of respondents' parents were living in either council or housing association rented accommodation, another third were owner-occupiers. Only two were in privately rented housing (possibly the most insecure type).

Given the long-established links between poverty, social class and ill health[29] it is not surprising that most families were tenants in rented accommodation and few were in higher level (higher paid) employment.

Since none of the parents who were ill or disabled were in employment we tried to establish what their jobs had been before they became unable to work. A small number, eight in total, had been in professional or managerial jobs such as nursing, teaching or other professions. Twelve had been employed in unskilled manual jobs, 11 in clerical or retail and 10 in skilled manual occupations. In the remaining cases the young people did not know what their parents'

occupational status had been. This was because they had either not worked since having children or had been ill since the respondents were young children and they could not remember.

PIE CHART 1: PARENTAL OCCUPATIONS PRIOR TO ILLNESS

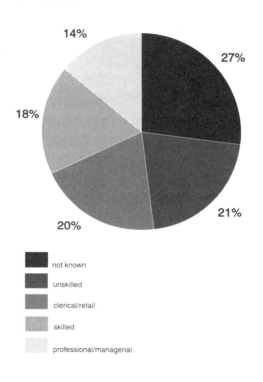

In the two-parent families we also tried to establish whether the second parent was in employment or what their job had been when they were. Only 11 out of 32 were still in employment. One was in a professional/managerial position, five in skilled manual work, four in unskilled work and one in retail/clerical. The rest were not in work and the young people didn't know what their jobs had been. Six were reported to be 'unemployed' although it was not clear whether they were seeking employment.

PIE CHART 2: SECOND PARENTS' OCCUPATION

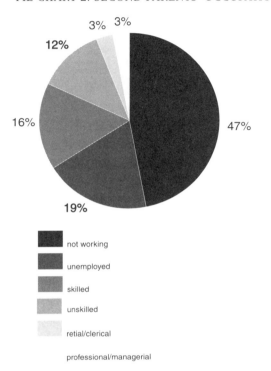

- not working
- unemployed
- skilled
- unskilled
- retial/clerical
- professional/managerial

Of those second parents not in employment, six had given up work specifically to become carers for their partners. Five of the six had been in unskilled work; one had been a professional but the necessity to care had coincided with redundancy. Type and level of employment (and pay) appears to be a critical factor, since it is probably financially viable to give up low paid, unskilled work more readily than a better paid job that might protect the family from poverty. It is therefore possible that in some families a second parent who can continue to work can protect children and young people from poverty. However, this protection from poverty may be at the expense of young people adopting caring roles since the absence of the second parent may leave young people to perform many caring tasks unaided. The onset of illness or disability may therefore cause many families to make crucial decisions, based on divisions of labour, both inside and outside the home, and financial considerations.

In many cases a (second) parent becoming a full-time carer will reduce the level of support provided by children and young people. However, this does depend upon the severity of the illness or disability and the availability and health of the second parent. For example, of those parents who gave up work to become full-time carers, two had since developed illnesses themselves. One had a stroke and herself required care (therefore increasing their daughter's caring role for both of them), another developed back problems as a result of lifting his partner, therefore their son became more involved in the heavier domestic tasks around the house. In two other cases the nature and severity of the illness meant that the young people remained heavily involved in caring and supporting their parents although they were not their primary carers. In one case the young woman's father had a degenerative disease which ultimately led to his death. As his condition deteriorated he required total care which she shared with her mother, his main carer. In another case, the young woman's mother had Alzheimer's Disease, which meant she required 24-hour care and could never be left alone. Inevitably she and her father shared the caring role, even though he was the main carer and did not go out to work. In cases such as these, the primary carer still required significant help from other family members because the condition was a progressive or degenerative one and care needs increased over time.

Caring relationships

Two-thirds of the young people in both age groups were caring for mothers and seven were caring for more than one person; either both parents, or a parent and a grandparent. These findings are similar to the large-scale studies of young carers[30], which indicated that mothers were far more likely to be care recipients, particularly in lone parent families. In cases where young people were providing support to both parents, they had initially assisted one and, when subsequently the other had developed an illness or disability, had 'absorbed' that parent's support needs into their existing regimes. As indicated previously, one young woman was providing support to her grandfather, having also cared for her grandmother until she died some time earlier.

The nature of illness/disability

Some of the parents had very complex medical conditions and a combination of health problems making a simple categorisation rather difficult. Where this was the case we have tried to take the most significant health problem, as defined by the young people themselves. Two-thirds had physical health problems, such as multiple sclerosis, stroke, arthritis, cardiac problems, etc. Ten had mental health problems, such as manic depression and schizophrenia, and five were misusing alcohol or drugs. In approximately eight cases there was a combination of physical and mental health problems, both of which necessitated some level of support. The national surveys[31] indicated that around a third of care recipients had mental health problems (including drug or alcohol misuse) and the findings from this study are similar. The nature and severity of illness or disability has an impact on the level and type of support required.

Caring tasks

The young people performed a range of tasks to support their parents, tasks that were associated with the nature and severity of parental illness or disability. We have adopted the same categorisations as in the national surveys to allow for comparisons. Almost all were involved in *domestic tasks* to a greater or lesser extent, similar to the national survey where the 1997 figure for 16 to 18-year-olds was 81 per cent. Such tasks include cleaning, cooking, washing and ironing. While research into young carers has commented on the sometimes inappropriately high level of tasks undertaken by some children, the age group currently under study would be expected to take on additional domestic tasks to prepare them for adulthood and independence. The transition to adulthood generally depends upon young people becoming self-sufficient, and undertaking domestic labour in the home is an integral part of the process. However, in this study domestic roles had often been undertaken at a very early age. While becoming self-sufficient can increase independence, in some cases where parents rely on their children for domestic and caring tasks, it can *prolong* the young person's dependence, since young people may feel unable to leave the parental home, and can also impede the parent's own independence. The following quote is from a young woman whose mother had mental health problems and who misused alcohol:

'I'm the more mature one out of me and my sister, I ended up taking on the role of the parent, trying to cook, trying to feed us … I mean it was mainly cereal and jam sandwiches 'cause I couldn't cook 'cause I was only 9.' (Melanie, age 16)

Over half the sample were performing *general caring tasks*, defined as assisting with mobility, giving medications or nursing-type tasks such as dressing wounds, etc. Again, this is comparable to the national surveys where the 1997 figure for 16 to 18-year-olds performing such tasks was 68 per cent. While domestic tasks would and, many would argue should, be performed by all young people, those whose parents are fit and well will not usually perform general caring tasks such as these. One young man assisted his mother who had poorly controlled diabetes resulting in very regular hypoglycaemic attacks when she lost consciousness, going into a diabetic coma. When he was younger severe attacks always resulted in hospital visits for glucose injections but more recently he had been taught how to do this:

'They've come out with a kind of glucagon syringe, you give her one of them and about 10 minutes later she'll start to come round. [The injection is given] in her legs, in her arms, in her stomach, wherever really … I notice it before my mum does, it's like as if she was drunk or something. You could tell, you know, the way she'd talk, and she'd slur and then sometimes – it's different things each time. Sometimes she can just have a fit and then pass out, sometimes she'll just go into it [coma] straight away, or she'll just act as though she's drunk.' (Darren, age 19)

Personal care was being provided by 28 of the young people, 14 from each age group. The 1997 national figure for 16 to 18-year-olds was a third, whereas in this sample slightly over a third of the younger age group and over half of the older ones were providing this type of support. Research into young carers has confirmed that personal, intimate care is the type of care most disliked by both parents and children. It can be embarrassing and humiliating for both parties to have a teenage or slightly older child washing, bathing or toileting a parent or dealing with other personal needs. Personal care is most often associated with physical illness or disability although a small number of young people provided this type of support to parents with severe mental health difficulties or those misusing alcohol when their illness resulted in their becoming unable to perform basic personal hygiene tasks. Obviously, in most families where parents are fit and well, children will not be assisting them with personal hygiene – this happens only where parents are particularly ill and unable to do this for themselves and where there are no other alternatives. One young woman, 15 at the time, provided total care for her father following a severe stroke and his subsequent discharge from a nursing home. She was taught to do so by the nursing staff at the home:

'I went there [nursing home] from morning 'til night and they showed me how to lift him, use hoist, feed him through his belly 'cause he'd had the operation done [insertion of gastrostomy tube], wash his mouth out so he can feel, you know, feel some tastes in his mouth, so he's not all dried up, and … oh, pressure areas as well, because he couldn't move, he'd be sat down all the time. They showed me how to lift him out of bed into chair and from chair into bed and they showed me how to dress all his pressure areas … I had to dress 'em, I did that when I put him to bed, when I laid him on his side. And he lost his speech as well, he were just like murmuring sort of thing, he could say a few little words but not many. It affected just about everything.' (Sandra, age 19)

The provision of *emotional support* is most closely associated with carers of people with mental health problems[32] and one-third of the respondents were providing this type of support. It is difficult to quantify emotional support and where access to assessments is based on the provision of regular and substantial care, as in the Carers Act, those providing emotional support may often be overlooked or, worse still, excluded. Although the guidance to the Act does include those people providing support to people with mental health problems, in practice they are often excluded. However, emotional support and observing a parent's mental state and mood changes, particularly if it is a parent with mental health difficulties, can be very emotionally draining and tiring for family members. A young woman whose mother had manic depression clearly articulated the emotional distress of monitoring her mother's mental health to ensure her safety:

'The manic state – when I was younger I used to see a difference in my mum. One minute she'd be, as I called it, all level, then she'd go high, where she'd be singing and quite boisterous compared to the normal mum and that's when I started realising hang on a second, she's gonna be in bed tomorrow, or saying she wants to die, she wished the world would end, and all the usual seeing things, hearing things, whatever. That's when I had to make sure she was taking the right medication at the right time and not overtaking it, because it did happen a couple of times.' (Clare, age 20)

Another young woman, also with a mother with manic depression, found coping with practical chores much easier than providing emotional support:

'She stops washing and everything so I was like washing the clothes. I know it's not much really, just washing the clothes, and I didn't really mind … and like cooking and stuff, 'cause my mum just lets herself go, she doesn't even clean herself, she just loses … doesn't see herself as important and she just doesn't do anything. But I don't think that's very hard really, doing that, I mean I don't mind. It's when you're having to deal with all the psychological aspects of it, when you're having to sort of understand … and it's really hard … you know, when people say really strange things and you can't even try to understand it.' (Laura, age 17)

A final role which some of the young people adopted, in addition to one or more other caring roles, was helping to care for younger siblings. Ten of the sample were involved in *childcare* and most were in the younger age group. This is clearly influenced by age; as young people get older so do their siblings and, once they reach 19 and above few have siblings young enough to require their care.

It is clear that the young people involved in the research come from a range of backgrounds and family situations and perform a variety of tasks for themselves, their parents and other family members. Each respondent is unique and has her or his own story to tell. Nevertheless they also share the experience of growing up with a parent or carer with an illness or disability and many of these young people's experiences are remarkably similar.

Summary of key findings

- 36 respondents were aged 16 to 18; 24 aged 19 to 25.
- Most were women; 24 in the younger age group, 21 in the older group.
- Only four were from minority ethnic communities.
- Half were living in lone parent families.
- One-third of parents were owner-occupiers; most were in rented accommodation.
- None of the parents who were ill or disabled were in employment; most had been in manual occupations.
- In two-parent families about a third of (second) parents were in employment; most in manual occupations.
- Two-thirds of respondents were caring for mothers; seven were caring for more than one person.
- Two-thirds of parents had physical health problems; one-third had mental health problems.
- Most young people were performing domestic tasks; over half were providing general care; almost half were providing personal care; one-third were offering emotional support; a few were caring for younger siblings in addition to one or more caring responsibilities.

3 Education, training and employment

Education and training

Education and qualifications are the main routes into employment, which marks the transition in status from student to employee. Furthermore, 'education is probably the most important route out of disadvantage and is a means of breaking cycles of deprivation'[33]. Research has often highlighted educational problems, a lack of time and energy for schoolwork and missed schooling as factors in the lives of many young carers[34].

Educational difficulties and missed school

Larger scale studies have confirmed that young carers often have educational problems. In the 1995 national survey of young carers, a third of all 5 to 15-year-olds and 42 per cent of 11 to 15s missed some school or experienced educational difficulties as a result of caring[35]. While there was some improvement between 1995 and 1997, the figures remain high at 28 per cent of all 5 to 15s and 35 per cent of 11 to 15-year-olds in the 1997 survey[36]. The large numbers of young carers of secondary school age who were missing school or experiencing some educational difficulties (indicated by receipt of educational welfare services, educational psychology or referral to specialist projects by educationalists) are clearly at risk of low educational achievement which may have knock-on effects once they leave school and enter further education or the labour market.

Since the majority of research into young carers has concentrated on those aged 18 and under it has been difficult to ascertain the extent to which educational problems at an early age will affect young people as they get older. However, the findings from this study confirm that missed education is a critical factor for many young people with ill or disabled parents. Furthermore, and perhaps more worrying, many of the young people who have a history of poor school attendance achieved no formal qualifications. Some were not even entered for examinations by their schools. One can only speculate as to the reasons for this, but school league tables may be a factor since not entering weaker students removes the possibility of their results lowering averages. However, some young people had effectively excluded themselves from being entered for examinations because of their poor attendance. In some cases they had (illegally) left school long before they were due to sit examinations or had not completed essential course work.

Of the 16 to 18-year-olds, 20 out of 36 had missed some school and 10 had no GCSEs. In the older age group, 11 out of 24 had missed school and five had no GCSEs. These figures are even higher than those from the national surveys and confirm that poor educational performance and achievement are common among young carers. Nationally, 5 per cent of the total school population are absent on any given day, while 2 per cent of Year 11 children truant for several weeks at a time, 2 per cent for several days at a time, and 34 per cent occasionally[37]. Clearly the findings from this study suggest that young carers were missing more school than most children. While some of these young people may have had little interest in education and might not have achieved significantly better results regardless of family circumstances, the majority confirmed that, in their view, missing school was a *direct result* of their caring roles. In some cases this was because young people were reluctant to leave parents alone, particularly when they were in pain, or feeling 'low' or depressed. In a small number of cases parents, especially those with mental health problems, did not want their children to leave them and requested that they stay at home. Some periodically missed school because they were feeling tired and 'stressed'.

For example, in one case a young man felt he had good reason to fear leaving his father. He had left him alone on one previous occasion when he had fallen from his wheelchair and fractured his hip. His reluctance to risk another accident resulted in his leaving school at 15:

'I missed a lot of school because he [dad] wasn't well and I didn't like leaving him in case he fell over and he couldn't reach a phone or pull the cords ... I went to it [school] twice a week, that was it ... until Year 11 and then I just drew the line and told them to give me home tuition or I don't come at all. And I got my home tuition.' (Mark, age 16)

One young woman left school at 15 to care for her father who had suffered a severe stroke and required total nursing care. She knew that he may die and she was adamant that she wanted to look after him at home rather than have him cared for in a nursing home or hospital. Her educational welfare officer supported her decision:

'I left [school] at 15 and then went back once a week and then sort of stopped going ... my welfare officer, she knew ... she actually come with me to one of the meetings [with the hospital staff] ... when I were 15, 'cause I were still sort of at school, she come with me and she understood I wanted to look after him so she were all for it and goes "Well, we'll get it sorted".' (Sandra, age 19)

Another young woman, whose mother had manic depression, missed school every few months when her mother's condition deteriorated. She usually managed to catch up with schoolwork but circumstances prevented her from gaining any qualifications:

'I missed quite a lot of school. I missed like, well senior school basically, I missed most of the senior stuff but I seemed able to catch up on the work and I was doing quite well. I studied for my GCSEs and that ... but at the time of the exams me mum was ill again and she was in hospital again and it was ... as she was getting better they used to send her home for day visits and it was like the days that she was being sent home were either a day when I had to have an exam or I had to revise for an exam. So it just happened that I only managed to sit about three of the exams but for the subjects that I took there was two exams for each subject and I only managed to take one of each so I never ended up getting any qualifications.' (Jane, age 19)

One young man simply did not like to leave his father alone for long periods of time:

'I went in and I said "I can't come in school 'cause I need to help my dad" and they say "As long as you're in for your exams you're OK" which is fair enough. Basically I don't want to leave him – the school understands why – when I first joined the school I said "My dad's disabled so I'm going to have a lot of time off" and so they try and help as much as they can.' (Ben, age 16)

In another rather extreme case, a young woman didn't attend school from age 5 to 10 because her mother had severe mental health problems and simply did not send her:

> 'I never went to school or anything, we just used to be in the house. We were really neglected actually … I didn't have any contact with any young people at all until about – it was when I started living with my grandma when I was about 10 and a half. When I went, well it was really bad actually. When I went to live with my grandma I didn't know my alphabet or anything. I had to learn, it was purgatory. Like my grandma was going through, making me do all this work every day and I had to learn my times tables.' (Laura, age 17)

The same young woman returned to living with her mother although she spent several periods in local authority care or the care of her grandparents. Unfortunately she too had problems getting qualifications:

> 'When she got ill it was at the time of my mocks [GCSEs] and I didn't want to leave at all, me and my sister, so we didn't … we used to miss days off school and everything … I didn't do my GCSEs. After my mocks I went back a year.'

It is evident that it some cases education welfare and teaching staff colluded with young people in their absence from school, perhaps in the mistaken belief that this was the most supportive course of action. While young people did not want a punitive approach to be taken, there must be a balance between supporting families and ensuring that children receive the education to which they are entitled. There must also be a balance between condoning and colluding with regular school

absences and recognising that, under certain circumstances, children may require support to stay at home. For example, where a parent has a terminal illness and may die soon, children and young people may be better supported at home to enable them to spend time with their parent. This is very different from children regularly missing school because of a lack of support in the home or because their parent does not want to be left alone.

Further and higher education

Given the large proportion of the sample that did miss school and fail to gain qualifications it is perhaps remarkable how many of them have persevered in education. Ten of the younger age group were still in school or sixth-form college, 13 of this age group and two of the older ones were in some form of further education, either taking or retaking GCSEs, doing vocational courses or doing A-levels.

Two of the older age group were at university, another had completed her degree and graduated with first class honours, and another was at university but had deferred her studies for a year as a result of severe depression following her father's death. One young woman had begun a university course but had not completed it because she found it difficult to cope with being too far away from her sick mother. This young woman's mother had since died.

While the numbers in further education may, at first sight, seem quite promising, suggesting a 'second chance' for many of those who achieved no or minimal educational success at school, they may simply disguise the lack of job opportunities for young people. Those job opportunities may also be further reduced because of missed education and limited qualifications.

While critical decisions have to be made at 16 regarding education, employment or training, the decrease in employment opportunities has made the alternatives to education much more risky[38]. The unemployment rate for 16 to 24-year-olds is almost double that of adults and one in four of all those unemployed and claiming benefits are under 25[39]. With the collapse of the youth labour market since the 1970s the government response has been to vocationalise education and develop new forms of training. Thus, the number in education may reflect a lack of viable alternatives rather than active choices.

Youth training

The Youth Training scheme (YTS) was introduced in 1983 and extended to two years in 1986. Changes to social security benefit rules in 1988 introduced an element of compulsion to such schemes and it is now very difficult for 16 to 18-year-olds to claim any form of welfare benefits. It is therefore surprising that only two of the younger age group were doing any form of youth training and a further two were about to begin a scheme. However, some of those who were at the point of completing compulsory education may have since become trainees. It has been suggested that 'school leavers are now virtually compelled to take part in post-school training schemes in place of either unemployment or a full-time job'[40]. It may be that this sample of young people deviates from the norm in this respect, but an alternative explanation is that the courses offered in FE colleges are more attractive to young people and seen as offering better qualifications than YT schemes. Teachers and careers advisers also influence young people, and FE courses appear to be suggested with more frequency than training schemes. A further possible explanation may be the amount of time that many young carers have

off school and college. Since there is no or little financial support, there are fewer sanctions for non-attendance than on a YT scheme that attracts an allowance. Courses may also be less than full-time leaving time for caring and domestic duties.

Financial hardship

One of the drawbacks of FE courses, unlike traineeships, is that they do not attract a training allowance. The young people who were involved in vocational training courses in FE colleges were, for the most part, without any form of income. A few received small grants from the local authority, but these do not compare favourably with YT training allowances. The lowest local authority grant was under £100 a term, the highest slightly over £400. While education may be a route out of poverty in the longer term, for many of these young people and their families it merely extended and exacerbated poverty. In some cases part-time work was possible and greatly increased the young people's independence from parents. In others, however, it was difficult to balance study, caring responsibilities and part-time work as well. Given that many of the young people had found it difficult to attend school regularly, some were unable to balance the triple responsibilities of work, home and study.

Graham (case 1, Chapter 1) was doing a college course and had no personal money at all:

'My mum gives me two quid for those three days [when in college] … it's from her social, from her social security … I mean mum does buy stuff from shopping for us but no, we don't, I mean some weeks, you know, say like one in every four weeks she can afford to give us like two quid. Well that's enough.'
Graham, age 16)

Although this young man was only in college for three days a week, he felt unable to find part-time work as his mother had a progressive, possibly terminal illness and required a considerable amount of support.

Another young woman who was at college was desperate for some money of her own as she felt unable to even eat properly because the family was poor. Her mother had run up credit card debts and then had to take out a loan to clear these debts, which exacerbated their poverty. Although she had been working part-time she had given up work when her mother had an operation and required additional support at home. When asked if there was anything she would like to change she replied: 'Be able to get pocket money. Stop mum [going into debt], go "Mum, you ain't having an Access card".'

Despite the financial hardships which studying brought for many young people, the rewards were viewed in terms of better job prospects and the ability to compete more evenly in the market for jobs. One additional advantage of the new vocationalism is that even those who leave school with no or minimal qualifications can attain NVQs and GNVQs which gives them a sense of achievement.

Employment

Ethnicity, gender and age are all factors that can be disadvantageous in the labour market. Many theories on labour markets take for granted that 'youth' is a particular stage in the life course and differentiate between youth and adult employment[41]. Social security law emphasises this distinction, allowing no benefits to 16 to 18-year-olds except under exceptional circumstances, and reduced benefits to under 25s. The minimum wage legislation, introduced while this study was in progress, perpetuates the divisions between older and younger workers, again making assumptions about the needs (and deserts) of younger people.

Aside from those engaged in part-time work while studying, only 10 of the older age group and five of the younger were in employment, one of each age group being employed under the New Deal arrangements. Two of those in the older age group were hoping to start university in the next academic year and one of these was only employed part-time. Thus, in the 19 to 25 age group, only seven were fully engaged in the labour market. One of the younger group had previously been her parent's full-time carer, although not in receipt of invalid carers allowance (ICA) and two of the older ones had previously been full-time carers and received the benefit.

The low number of respondents who were fully engaged in the labour market reflects recent trends for longer and less straightforward transitions. While in the past work was the traditional route into adulthood, particularly for working-class young people, with higher education providing an alternative route for middle-class children, patterns are now more complex.

The oil crisis in the 1970s, high levels of unemployment and the collapse of the youth labour market greatly reduced opportunities for young people. The policy responses to these crises have been to extend the period of transition by increasing the school leaving age and reducing eligibility to social security benefits. Alongside the increased emphasis on education and training rather than employment, have come the erosion of student grants and the introduction of loans and tuition fees. Such policies push dependency back onto families and make independence and the transition to adulthood more difficult to achieve.

However, employment has always been the route into independence and an income the way in which people exercise choices and participate fully in society. Not only does economic independence enable full participation, but also 'leaving home, getting married and other transition events associated with adulthood have depended upon getting a job'[42]. The increased emphasis on families taking responsibility for young people does not take into account the difficulties faced by many families, for example, poverty, poor health, the need for support and care. Nor does it take into account the needs of young people who, for whatever reason, are unable (or unwilling) to rely on their families for such support. In families that are reliant on welfare benefits (and the majority of the respondents' families were in just such a position), these policies can cause greater hardship.

Young people who have ill or disabled parents who require their support may be less available for work and more likely to have fewer and lower educational qualifications. Rather than making the transition into employment and financial independence they may be more prone to transitions into unemployment. Of the sample, five of the younger and four of the older age group were unemployed although one of the younger ones was about to start a YT scheme. One of the older age group who was in employment worked on a casual basis and therefore occasionally moved into unemployment if no work was available.

Changes to social security rules make it almost impossible for 16 to 18-year-olds to claim benefits if unemployed. Of the five who were not in work, education or training one had never worked nor tried to claim benefits, relying on his mother for financial support. Another had given up a college course and was seeking work, while one was about to start a YT scheme. One young woman had mental health problems herself and was unable to work – she had not tried to claim benefit, again relying on her family for financial support. Another acted as her mother's full-time carer but had not tried to claim ICA and was looking for part-time work that she felt she would be able to combine with caring for her mother.

In the older age group two of those not in work were lone parents living independently from their families and were both claiming income support (IS) and housing benefit. A third was also living independently and claiming jobseeker's allowance (JSA). The other one had deferred her university course due to ill health and was claiming IS. While it is easier for people in this age group to claim benefits, rates are lower than for the over 25s.

Full-time carers claiming ICA

Finally, three of the older age group were full-time carers in receipt of ICA, and a fourth was claiming ICA while studying at university. All of these were young women. ICA is one of the few benefits that younger people can claim (and at the same rate as over 25s) providing they and the person in receipt of care meet the eligibility criteria.

Two of these young women had never entered the full-time labour market. One was in college part-time while assisting her disabled mother. When she became pregnant she couldn't manage to continue with study, caring and parenthood and, since her mother requires a high level of care, she began to claim the benefit. She had never tried to claim before this time. Karen (case 4, Chapter 1) provided care and support to her mother while at school and college but when she was hoping to take a year out and move away, her grandmother had a stroke. Her mother and grandmother both required her support and so she too had never entered the labour market, nor had the opportunity to go to university as she had intended.

One of those in receipt of ICA had entered the labour market but required time off work at quite regular intervals in order to offer support to her mother and father. Her employers were unhappy and so she became a full-time carer. The other case was quite unusual since her claim was originally rejected once she became an undergraduate. She appealed successfully against the ruling as her full-time university course involved only a small amount of contact teaching time:

> 'Well I'm only in university eight hours a week and I said although it's classed as a full-time course, I do less work at university than I did at A-levels when I was doing 18 hours a week. I got in touch with someone from the welfare department from university and I fought and fought and fought and got it to a tribunal.'
> (Julie, age 21)

Analysing the situations and experiences of the respondents indicates that transitions from school to employment or training are complex and influenced by many factors including caring responsibilities. Educational experiences and outcomes were sometimes very negative for those young people who had parents who required care, particularly when their parents received inadequate social care provision and lived on a low income. This placed them at a disadvantage in relation to both further education and employment. Policies that promote family responsibilities are contradictory. On the one hand community care legislation emphasises the caring responsibilities of families. However, on the other hand, legislation which has eroded student grants, introduced loans and tuition fees, reduced benefits to under 25s, removed eligibility to benefits for most 16 to 18-year-olds, and introduced a reduced minimum wage for younger workers, results in parents having to support their children for longer and longer periods.

However, families have changed and lone parents now head many. When lone parents require support through illness or disability there is little provision available since assumptions are made regarding familial duties and responsibilities. Even where there are two parents few families can afford to survive financially without an income, resulting in children adopting roles that may be inappropriate and may transgress norms.

Young people can no longer make a direct transition from school to work, but are required to undergo training, which does not attract a wage but an allowance. This period of training may be followed by another period where they earn less than the minimum wage, or claim reduced benefits. It may therefore make financial sense for some young people to adopt caring roles in families where they are unable to make adequate financial contributions. However, this will make future transitions all the more difficult since educational qualifications and work experience are almost essential for a positive transition. This is a 'Catch 22' position for many young carers.

Caring for one's parents is not a new phenomenon, but recent policy changes coupled with the way in which childhood is viewed – as a time of dependence – make it more hidden than would have previously been the case.

> 'The context in Britain in the early decades of this century was one where young adult children were likely to have many more

obligations to their parental household, both financial and caring, than is typical in the post-war period.'[43]

This research suggests that we are not as far removed from these early decades as we would like to think.

Summary of key findings

- A large proportion of young carers had educational problems and missed school. Many failed to attain any educational qualifications.
- Education welfare and teaching staff often colluded in young carers' absence from school.
- A lack of educational qualifications combined with ongoing caring responsibilities served to exclude some young carers from the labour market.
- In the absence of education maintenance allowances and labour market opportunities, continuing to care appeared understandable in some families. However, this served to deny some young carers a step into the competitive labour market and transition to financial independence. It also put them at a disadvantage in the future as they competed against people who were younger, qualified and cheaper to employ.

4 Cash and care: Income, benefits and services

An adequate income, as we saw in the previous section, enables full participation in society and is the means through which many of the factors associated with transition to adulthood, such as spatial and financial independence, are achieved. In relation to ill or disabled people, an adequate income enables them to pay for appropriate care and support, reducing the need to rely on family members. People who, through illness or disability, are unable to perform tasks associated with daily living require adequate support and care services. However, illness, disability and poverty tend to go hand-in-hand[44] and conversely those families most likely to require social care and support are those least able to afford it. It is the combination of adequate cash and care that enables ill or disabled people to maintain their independence and participate more fully in society.

Income and benefits

When assessing young people's transitions to adulthood, both family and individual incomes are important to ensure social inclusion. An independent income allows young people to act as consumers in their own right and to move towards becoming financially independent of their parents, while an adequate family income protects the whole family from poverty and can subsidise young people until they can earn enough to become self-sufficient.

Income is usually derived from paid employment but illness and disability make employment more difficult. Disabled people generally suffer discrimination in the labour market and those with chronic, long-term illness are often unable to work. In the section on respondents' characteristics we saw that none of the parents with illness or disability was in employment and, where they had partners, few of these were working.

With two exceptions, all of the families were in receipt of some form of welfare or disability benefits. The most commonly received benefit was disability living allowance (DLA), sometimes in combination with income support. DLA is a benefit paid to people who are under 65 when they apply. It has two components, a care component and a mobility component – which most respondents referred to as 'mobility allowance'. The mobility component is for people who have difficulty getting around, the care component for people with care or supervision needs. Both components are paid at different rates depending on circumstances. DLA is not based on National Insurance contributions. Income Support is a benefit for people with a low income who are not in full-time paid work. It too is not based on National Insurance contributions.

Receipt of income support can be taken as a proxy indicator of poverty since it is paid as a top-up to those families whose level of income or benefit is deemed inadequate. Ten families were definitely in receipt of IS; six of them were receiving it in addition to some other disability benefits. Understandably not all of the young people were sure which benefits their parents received; four thought it was definitely a form of disability benefit while seven just knew there were some benefits coming into the family.

It is clear from the findings that few of the families were in the position of having sufficient income to purchase services and increase their independence. Only one parent was receiving money from the Independent Living Fund (ILF), which she used to employ two personal assistants, and none appeared to be receiving direct payments. The 1996 Direct Payment Act allows social services departments to make direct payments to some people who have been assessed as requiring social care services. While the money can only be used to purchase services assessed as needed, it does offer people the flexibility of purchasing and arranging services to meet their and their families' needs. Nearly all the families, however, were reliant on services arranged by local social services departments.

The previous chapter shows that only 15 of the young people were in employment, two of whom were intending starting university in the next academic year. Of those not in employment, most were still living in the parental home and most were reliant on their parents for money. There were one or two exceptions where the young person received some benefit in their own right but, as we saw previously, it is very difficult for young people to access the benefit system. None of those who were in education and had part-time jobs received any money from their parents.

Three of the young people who were in employment were living independently of their parents and therefore not contributing to the family income. Jones and Wallace[45] suggest that while at 17 the cash flow within families is from parent to child, by 19 it is from child to parent as young people enter the labour market and begin to contribute to the family resources. However, this study clearly indicates that few young carers were in a position to be able to make financial contributions. Jones and Wallace[46] also suggest that financial support in later teenage years is more often associated with middle-class young people. However, a large number of our respondents were in further education, and therefore financially dependent on families regardless of socio-economic or class status. Some of the respondents who were still living with their parents spoke about the problems of living on low incomes:

> 'I just don't eat healthy food, we ain't got the money to eat healthy food.' (Gill, age 17)

> '[I eat] anything I can lay my hands on at the moment 'cause we haven't got much in … sometimes we can live on toast for a week.' (Judy, age 16)

Those living independently also experienced financial difficulties:

> 'It's [financial outgoings] just mainly household bills and I've got like catalogue bills and I've got a loan off the Provident because before Christmas I was finding it difficult to get money for like food and that because you've got to buy extra food and presents for people. Because the money I'm on is just enough for me to live on, it's not enough for anything else really.' (Jane, age 19)

> 'I have to pay £7 towards my rent. Food, cigarettes and it doesn't go far at all. The housing benefit pays £70 of my rent. With this being a hostel – it's one of the cheapest ones – that includes gas, electric, TV licence … most of the time I don't buy food because I can't afford it … I at least have, I think, four proper meals a week … nothing [for going out] the only way I can actually spend money on myself is if I don't buy cigarettes and food.' (Melanie, age 16)

A second parent's income protected some families, but most were lone parent families and had been for a long time. Lone parents are much more likely to experience poverty and these particular parents were unable to take employment because of their health difficulties.

Services

About a third of the respondents' parents had on-going support, either social care services such as home care, or mental health specific services such as community psychiatric nurses (CPN). Approximately one-fifth had had their homes adapted in some way to make them more accessible for the disabled parent. This usually involved the provision of a lift, a shower, or doors widened and kitchen surfaces lowered for wheelchair users. However, a third had no on-going services at all. There were a variety of reasons for this, but refusal or cancellation of services by families was much more common than refusal to provide on the part of social services.

Sometimes either parent, young person or both found services intrusive and preferred to be left alone:

'Social services immediately put in place a care package with someone coming in at 8 o'clock in a morning, someone coming at 1 o'clock in the afternoon, to dress my mam, do whatever she needed. And that lasted not very long, because my mam … she didn't like it, it was very regimental, you know, so she was quite determined to get some normality back, so she did a lot, started doing things for herself and got the care package taken out ... I was a bit concerned that my mam was cutting things off, you know what I mean, and I thought well, if I know that I've got someone to ring, like her social worker, just to put it back into place if necessary.' (Diana, age 23)

'We had it [home care] once but didn't like it. What happened was, we said if you want to come, come, but they kept going into my bedroom and I don't like people going in there.' (Ben, age 16)

'She [mum] doesn't want one [care attendant]. To me it would be like someone prying into your personal life and everything.' (Sue, age 20)

'We had a home help, I don't know how long they lasted but, to be honest, I've seen them doing the jobs that I was doing and I didn't like strangers in the house. So that didn't last long. A few weeks it lasted, about a month at the most.' (Anna, age 19)

'She used to have them [community psychiatric nurses] she didn't want it no more … just wanted to be left alone.' (Sarah, age 16)

In other cases charges for services proved prohibitive:

'We had home help for ages but suddenly they just stopped. They wanted my mum to pay but she couldn't 'cause she had no money, so they stopped. [I felt] gutted. I was, like, "Oh no, not again".' (Judy, age 16)

'We had home help last year but all they did was hoover up. It was useless so we got rid of them. They came like an hour twice a week I think. And it was a fiver a week, just for hoovering … they were supposed to be helping my dad out but I used to come home like and used to move … not move, but you know, not have things like you left them. So you'd have to rearrange them when you got home.' (Janice, age 17)

'Well we have to pay for it [home care] so it's hard … it's double time on Friday, Saturday and Sunday.' (Mark, age 16)

'[I] think it was about three or four months [home care] and then they decided you had to pay for everything … she used to go round to a day centre but it's like I think it's about £40 for two days … it was just too much for what they were doing … they're [home care] getting paid for two hours and then they're not, they're not staying for two hours. But I'd rather do it all myself now that I'm used to doing it.'
(Kim, age 16)

Where services were provided sensitively, were acceptable to the family and were reliable and trusted, they could make a big difference to the lives of young people as well as their parents. Mike, for example, (case 3, Chapter 1) found that an increased care package that met his mother's personal care needs greatly reduced his own caring role:

'Before I was doing practically everything, now I'm practically redundant. Not so much all the housework, because she's always had the home care, I was doing the personal care. Now they're doing the home and personal care, coming visiting during the nights, just about everything.' (Mike, age 19)

Other young people had confidence in support services because staff were approachable and professional:

'Me dad had Tony and me mum had Sarah and they were lovely. I loved it, they were more friends than CPNs. And then when we moved

here, because the district is different, they had to get two new CPNs from over here, and that's Stuart and Carol and I can't stand them. Like, with me mum being ill last Friday, she was going downhill and I rang her CPN and she went "I'll try and come out tomorrow". Now if I'd rung Sarah or the crisis team in [town] they would've come out the same day.'
(Debbie, age 18)

'I only met the psychiatric social worker and she never really used to say anything to me and tell me what was going off, but I knew, I had that confidence that she was there helping, even though she didn't say it to me, I knew.'
(Laura, age 17)

During 1998 and 1999 the Social Services Inspectorate (SSI) conducted a series of inspections of various local authorities' services to support disabled adults in their parenting role. From these inspections[47] it is clear that few local authorities have *specific* policies relating to disabled parents and that disabled people's personal care needs take priority over their needs as individuals and as parents. Furthermore, while local authorities promote a social model of disability, staff are often unsure of what this actually means in practice. An example of a positive approach to supporting parents is Employment Options Inc. in America[48], where parents with mental health problems are supported through a variety of services such as parenting education, home visits, service coordination and visitation support for parents without custody. None of the young carers' parents appeared to have any similar parenting support. The cancelling of services by families may therefore be a result of parental needs not being taken fully into account, and a concentration by service providers on personal care needs rather than the needs of disabled people as parents.

It is clear that illness and disability reduce autonomy and force many families to be reliant on welfare benefits and support services arranged by third parties. Services that are too expensive or deemed intrusive are less likely to be acceptable to families resulting in young people adopting additional roles and responsibilities. It is possible that if services were provided early, families may become accustomed to them and be less likely to cancel them. Once young caring has become established families appear to be more likely to deem services intrusive and young people prefer to perform tasks themselves and in their own way. Graham, for example (case 1, Chapter 1), did not want anyone to take over what he viewed as his tasks. Early interventions should therefore prevent caring by children from becoming established and institutionalised. Services that are affordable, adaptable and acceptable can greatly improve the lives of all family members and reduce the caring responsibilities adopted by children and young people. These services should support disabled adults as parents as well as supporting their personal care needs. Perhaps the way forward is early assessment of the needs of *whole* families. Currently community care assessments tend to be done during working hours when any children in the family should be at school. Ensuring that all family members can be present and included in discussions (while recognising disabled parents' and children's rights to privacy and confidentiality) should assist social services in recognising and meeting disabled parents' needs as both parents and people with an illness or disability. Furthermore, the needs and rights of children within the family must also be considered to ensure that they do not adopt inappropriate roles nor feel undermined by the provision of services. Family-focused assessments should acknowledge and recognise the needs and rights of all family members and should lead to the provision of services which meet these needs and promote these rights.

Summary of key findings

- Virtually all the families were in receipt of welfare benefits and were outside the paid labour market. Experience of poverty and social exclusion was common.
- While some families did receive helpful and valued services, one-third received nothing at all and some had cancelled services that they viewed as intrusive, unnecessary, poor quality or too expensive.
- Once young caring became established families were more likely to cancel services.
- Where families received good quality and reliable support and services this reduced young people's caring roles.
- There was no evidence of any services specifically to support disabled parents in their parenting role.

5 Leaving home: Permanent and temporary transitions

Leaving home is an important stage in the transition to adulthood that usually requires financial independence from one's parents, although not necessarily from the state. In contrast, temporary transitions, such as going to university, tend to be increasingly dependent upon parental financial support. For a successful transition, young people require not only access to a sufficient income (either from earnings or benefits) but also the skills and competencies that will enable them to live independently. The section on respondents' characteristics demonstrates the extent to which the young people in the study are involved in domestic tasks, and later we will see that many viewed this as good preparation for independence. Young carers demonstrate many of the life skills necessary for successful spatial transitions. However, as we will indicate, this is often at considerable cost.

Some of the young people in the study had left home to live independently, some had left home and then returned, some had firm plans to leave the parental home in the immediate future, while others had temporarily left home, or were about to go to university. In addition, some had experienced family separation as a result of local authority care proceedings or informal arrangements where they moved in with family, friends or neighbours.

Leaving home and becoming independent

Seven of the respondents had left home to live independently; one was married with a child, two were lone parents. Of the seven, one was living in shared accommodation, one in a hostel for homeless women and the remaining five were in rented accommodation, either housing association or council. The three with children were all in secure rented accommodation.

In five cases out of the seven, the move away from parents was not the result of a planned and positive choice. One young woman moved into a hostel for homeless women, as she could no longer face living at home. Housing benefit paid her rent. Her mother had mental health problems and misused alcohol and she, the daughter, had an eating disorder and was harming herself. She felt this was a direct result of her home situation. She was desperate to leave and had asked to be taken into care or fostered but was considered too old. She commented:

'My youth worker told me about this house [hostel] because she knew how desperate I was to get out of home and because I'd turned 16, it was like, I can move out, but where? Because the housing association won't give you a flat of your own at 16.' (Melanie, age 16)

Another young woman whose mother also had mental health problems reached crisis point when she left home at 16. Housing benefit also paid her rent:

'Things had been going bad for about 10 months with my mum's health problems. I was getting to the stage where I knew if I stayed there that I would end up ending my life, never mind hers … It had been the worst weekend of my life, she was, I can't explain it, she admits now it was one of the scariest for her while she's been mentally ill, as well. She was seeing things and hearing things, she was following me every-where. … I phoned the young carers project, I said "I'm not going back to that flat again, ever. I don't consider it to be a home". I said "I don't

care what happens but I'm not going home".'
(Clare, age 20)

This particular young woman stayed with a teacher during her GCSEs and then with extended family members (who also had health problems) before finally, at 17, getting a flat of her own.

In another case – again a young woman whose mother had mental health problems and misused alcohol – a social worker arranged hostel accommodation when she was 16 and she was allocated a council flat at 17. She was in full-time employment and paid her own rent:

'I just had to decide myself that even though I loved my mum and cared a lot about her and was worried about her, I just didn't want to live with her any more, I wanted to live on my own. Still go to visit her and at least if I went to see her and if it got out of hand and she got too drunk and got violent I could walk away and come back to where I was living.'
(Hannah, age 18)

In another case the move was not precipitated by a crisis but the respondent felt it was possibly earlier than it might have been had she not been supporting her mother. She was, however, prepared to continue to offer support at a distance, which was only achieved by leaving home. She gave up college and worked full-time to enable her to pay her own rent:

'She knows she can phone me if she needs anything … providing she doesn't insist I change my plans it doesn't bother me. If I can fit it around my schedule then fair enough because, yeah, they are my family. But I'm not living at home any more, I have my own life

away from it. I am not the back-up person any more.' (Lauren, age 18)

Two of the young people took over the council tenancies on their parents' homes. In one case the respondent's father died, and in the other the respondent's mother went into full-time care. Again, the choice was not an active one but was dictated by circumstances outside the young people's control.

Of the other two young people who were living independently, one was married and living with her partner and the other had left home to be alone with her child. Both expressed some guilt at leaving the family to cope without them.

One young woman was about to leave home to live with her boyfriend but intended to visit her parents every day and to continue to take full responsibility for her mother's care and the family domestic arrangements (cooking, cleaning, washing, ironing, etc). Karen (case 3, Chapter 1) talked about leaving 'when it was all over' referring to her grandmother's illness. The only possible way out for her would be her grandmother's death as her mother also has health problems and could not cope with her own mother without her daughter's help. Interestingly, two young men, both aged 16 and caring for fathers with physical disabilities, never intended leaving and both said that, should they become involved in a serious relationship, they would expect their partners to move into the family home with them. None of the young women mentioned having partners move into the parental home, although the boyfriend of one was staying with her family while the couple awaited more suitable housing. Young women were more likely to defer relationships or try to fit them alongside family responsibilities.

Temporary transitions

Temporary transitions from the parental home included those who had left, or were about to leave, to go to university and those who had left and returned to the parental home.

Two respondents were currently at university, one had completed her degree, another had terminated her studies before graduating and the fifth had suspended her studies. Four respondents were intending to start at university in the next academic year. Some of these young people had been influenced by family factors. For example, one of the current students and two of those about to start at university had restricted their choices to more local universities to either enable them to live at home or to be close enough to go home at weekends. The one who terminated her studies had done so because her mother was very ill and she felt unable to continue studying while her father and sister coped alone. She returned to the family home and helped to care for her mother until she died. The one who had suspended her studies had done so as a result of depression following her father's death.

Clearly the provision of adequate services is a factor which influences choices in education: the mother of the current student who lived away from home had a live-in carer, whereas the current student who lived at home was classed as her mother's carer and was in receipt of ICA. Those who wanted to stay reasonably close felt that their support would be beneficial to their parents, even on a temporary weekend basis.

In addition to those temporarily living away from home for educational purposes there were five who had left and then returned to the family home. Two of the five related their moving out to the caring situation. In one case, having cared for the whole family, in particular her younger siblings, for an extended period one young woman experienced conflict with her mother. Once her mother began to regain strength and her condition improved, the young woman found it difficult to relinquish the role she had adopted. The younger siblings came to her with requests rather than their mother and the situation became difficult for both parties. After staying away for a few months she returned home. She felt she and her mother benefited from the break but was quick to point out that: *'It wasn't like I'd left my mum in the lurch because she's a lot more independent and things.'* This young woman was planning to move out again, but this time the move would be planned and, hopefully for her, permanent.

The other respondent who left indirectly because of parental illness felt that her mother became argumentative when her manic depression was poorly controlled. She found living with the uncertainty of mental ill health difficult and resented the arguments between her and her mother and between her parents, which she saw as a direct result of her mother's mental health problems. She left for a few months, staying with friends, and continued to spend a lot of time with friends when her mother was unwell. She would have liked to leave permanently as soon as possible, but at the time of the interview was only 16 and still in school.

The other three had left for a variety of reasons. Two had tried unsuccessfully to live with estranged fathers and the third had personal problems. Of the two who moved to be with fathers, one lived in a hostel before returning home. In the other case, the woman's mother was rehoused into a one bedroom flat (one of the reasons for the move). When things did not work out with her father she returned home at the same time as her brother. All three were living in the one bedroom flat awaiting more suitable accommodation.

Formal and informal care arrangements

Parental illness is the third most common reason for children entering the public childcare system[49] and three of the respondents had been in care at some time in their lives. Although there is no specific literature on children looked after because of parental ill health, where it is mentioned, it is usually in relation to *mental* ill health. Two of the three were taken into care because their parents' mental health problems necessitated hospital admissions. This was true of Sharon (case 2, Chapter 1):

'I was in foster care, my brother went in foster care as well, in '90, between '91 and '94 I think, on and off, in and out of care … because my dad had a drinking problem between then, and depression and stuff like that.' (Sharon, age 17)

One young woman was not aware that her mother's partner was in fact her stepfather rather than her biological father. It was only after several episodes of being in care that she discovered the truth:

'I used to go in foster care a lot then 'cause she started getting ill when I was about 9, with mental illness, and we were always swapping from one foster home to another. And then I met my dad when I was about 11 and my mum was really ill then, so I lived with my [paternal]

grandparents for four years and then I moved back with my mum.' (Laura, age 17)

This same young woman vividly recalled her anguish about making decisions relating to her mother's health, knowing what the consequences would be for her and her sister:

'Last time she was ill I don't know whether I did the right thing or not 'cause we could tell, 'cause she gets ill really quickly. And it was about two weeks and on the third week I rang – not the hospital – my mum's psychiatric social worker and told them to check up on my mum and everything. I don't know whether I should have just left it to progress or see to it as soon as possible. Because my mum went into hospital and then me and my sister had to go into foster care, and I feel as though it was all my fault. With my sister having to go through all that. And I don't know whether I should have left it or not. Because the time before that, when I was living with my grandparents and my mum was ill, my sister left it for months. She left my mum for months and my mum locked my sister in the house and my sister wouldn't tell anybody because she didn't want my mum to go into hospital.' (Laura, age 17)

Two other respondents had not been admitted to care, but social services had arranged for their neighbours to look after them while their mother, also with mental health problems and who misused alcohol, was in hospital. In fact, in one case the young woman concerned did not feel that this informal arrangement was in her best interest since, when she requested to be taken into care at 15 social services refused. She felt that if she had had a history of being in care that she would have got more support. Another young woman, again with a mother with mental health problems, was made a ward of court until the age of 14 and regularly cared for by her grandparents when her mother was ill.

Four other respondents had siblings who had been in care. None of them related this to parental illness, rather to behavioural difficulties, but it is interesting to note that in two cases one of the parents had mental health problems.

The study demonstrates that transitions to independence may be difficult and that young carers may leave home for a variety of reasons, often returning before making a permanent move. One of the problems for young leavers is that it is difficult to find a home when under the age of 18. The young woman living in a hostel commented on this:

'When they opened this hostel three years ago they were really only expecting people to stay here for probably between six to 12 months, probably not even that. But the applicants who they've actually had have been getting younger and younger, like 16, because you can't get put on the list until you're 17 and a half, which means that you can't really get a flat until you're about 18, 18 and a half. So I've probably got another year here unless the council gives me a flat … they can't actually put me on the waiting list until I'm 17.' (Melanie, age 16)

Changes in housing policy have exacerbated problems for young people wanting to live independently. The right-to-buy policy has removed a lot of social housing stock away from the rented sector and into private ownership. Young people are not seen as priorities for housing unless they have children.

While most of our respondents were happy to remain in the parental home, some, particularly those whose parents had mental health problems, found it difficult if not impossible to stay. Others deferred leaving home because they felt 'needed' at home. Clearly a combination of parental illness, lack of support services and a lack of available and affordable alternative accommodation can influence transitions to spatial independence.

Summary of key findings

- Leaving home was especially problematic for many young carers, particularly if they had to leave a parent who required considerable help and support. Some young people delayed this transition to spatial independence. Young carers who temporarily left home to study also restricted their choices, even if they didn't delay their departure.
- In families where a parent had a severe and enduring mental health problem, young carers' spatial transitions were sometimes premature and traumatic if, for example, the young person reached crisis point or had to be received into public care.

6 Becoming an adult: Young people's perspectives

We wanted to establish how young people felt their lives, decisions, choices, etc. had been influenced by providing support to a parent with an illness or disability – in both positive and negative ways. We were also interested in establishing what they felt were the important factors in moving into adulthood and whether they considered themselves to be adults.

The caring role: positive and negative impacts

Helping parents and other family members is an important part of growing up. Not only does it teach consideration for others and aid maturity and responsibility, but it also benefits young people as they make the transition from childhood to adulthood. The ability to perform domestic chores prepares children and young people for independence in later life. Assisting family members, both parents and younger siblings, prepares them for possible partnerships and parenthood. It is only when inappropriate roles are adopted, for example, personal, intimate care, or too much responsibility is taken on at too early an age, that the caring role can have negative impacts. However, even where inappropriate roles are not adopted, stress may still occur.

Stress and depression

Having a parent who is ill or disabled can itself be stressful. Seeing a parent in pain or with a progressive, debilitating illness can be very difficult for a child or young person. Some of the young people who we interviewed had already experienced the death of a parent, others were aware that their parents would die soon. In some cases the young people were at risk of developing disorders themselves. For example, one young man's mother had Huntington's Disease and he had received genetic counselling. A young woman whose mother had very early onset Alzheimer's Disease stated that, had she been at risk, she would have committed suicide rather than go through what she witnessed in her mother. Others spoke about being much more aware of their diet and lifestyles when their parents had heart disease and strokes.

Living with a parent with severe and enduring mental health problems can also cause considerable anxiety and stress. As we saw in a previous chapter, three respondents had left home very early as they felt they could no longer live with their mentally ill parents. Two had been in local authority care, two had alternative care arrangements made by social services and another was made a ward of court, all as a result of parental mental ill health. In each of these cases the young people were aware that it was their parent's illness which sometimes caused unpredictable or erratic behaviour, and not a lack of care and concern on their parent's part. Nevertheless, living with mental ill health for these young people meant living with unpredictability and uncertainty.

While many of the respondents spoke about feeling depressed and 'stressed out', a number had experienced health problems as a result of this stress. Five had been prescribed anti-depressants by a GP and another had been offered treatment but refused. In one of these cases the young woman had been admitted to hospital suffering from depression following her father's death. Five respondents reported eating disorders, either anorexia or bulimia, although only one had received medical treatment for this. Two had taken overdoses in the past and one had slashed her arms and wrists. Another had an ulcer caused, according to her, by stress. Only one respondent reported back problems as a result of lifting. It is clear that while many of the respondents (and many young people generally) find life stressful, in some cases this stress can be debilitating and can cause health problems.

When asked about specific advantages and disadvantages, or positive and negative points, related to assisting a parent with illness or disability the responses were quite varied. What some saw as advantageous others viewed in the opposite way.

Positive aspects

Many of the young people viewed the maturity, responsibility, independence and life skills they had acquired in a positive light. They could see that these would be useful to them throughout life and felt better prepared for adulthood than many of their peers. About a quarter of all the respondents mentioned these qualities as being the best part of helping to care for and support a parent who was ill or disabled.

Other comments on the positive nature of caring were gaining an understanding about illness and disability and having a caring attitude towards others. Seven respondents specifically mentioned the closeness of their relationships with their parents.

Negative aspects

As we indicated above, having an ill or disabled parent can be stressful and concern about parents' wellbeing was a central anxiety for many respondents. Six of the young people specifically felt that the worst thing was seeing parents ill, in and out of hospital or terminally ill. One respondent felt very lonely following the death of her father, four mentioned stresses and tiredness as the worst aspects of caring. Other responses related to the impact parents' illnesses had on the family as a whole, for example, not being able to do things other families did, such as go out and do activities, go on holiday,

etc. These outcomes are, of course, closely related to family income, not just illness and disability.

In the chapter on education, training and employment, we saw that young people had frequently missed school and that some had few educational qualifications. Four specifically mentioned restricted choices in education and career as one of the more negative aspects. Another common response was restricted time to oneself for socialising, going out and generally 'being a teenager'.

While many respondents viewed their level of maturity and responsibility in a positive light, six felt they had grown up too quickly and were mature beyond their years. However, some acknowledged the skills this maturity had brought and felt that although they had done too much too soon, these skills were now useful to them.

While several of the respondents commented on the closeness of their relationships with parents only one felt she had not had love and support from her mother.

Making choices: influences and restrictions

As we saw in the previous chapter, decisions to leave home, either permanently or temporarily, were sometimes influenced by concerns over parental ill health. Many of the respondents made the transition to independent living at an earlier or later stage than they would have chosen.

Perhaps the most important decisions which the young people felt had been influenced by parental illness, were those related to careers and jobs.

Sometimes choices were influenced by home experiences but restricted by lack of qualifications. One young woman originally wanted to be a home care worker but then changed her mind. She wanted a caring job since she felt she had the experience, but having left school at 15, had no qualifications:

> 'I thought home help because I'd looked after my dad so I knew I had experience in that, so that was another reason really. And then I thought well, childcare is still caring and I love kids so I'll go for that.' (Sandra, age 19)

Others also found that lack of qualifications restricted their choices:

> 'I originally wanted to do nursing and I talked to my careers thing and she said I had no chance of doing it because I've never passed my exams … nursery nursing I could have done. I was going to do health and social care but I talked about it to the careers woman at college and she said with your caring for your mum and all that you've done, it would probably just bore you to do the same thing again.' (Kirsty, age 16)

> 'I was enquiring about social work and social services and I know basically you've got to have this, you've got to have that, you've got to have the other. And I was like, "Oh my God, I haven't got none of those".' (Anna, age 19)

In both of the above cases the original choice of career had been influenced by personal experience but restricted by lack of qualifications – again a 'Catch 22' position.

Another young woman whose mother had mental health problems felt she could use her experiences to help others:

> 'I wanted to be a clinical psychologist at first, but I don't know whether to do that or whether,

I fancy the idea of being a teacher and doing counselling as well at the same time. But, I mean, you have to get really good grades … I just like working with people and I've had lots of experience in different sort of aspects of life really and I could relate to people really well with any problems they have.' (Laura, age 17)

One young man was helping to care for his mother who was disabled following polio as a child and then a brain haemorrhage some years ago. While he felt the family could manage without his support in relation to his mother, his father had recently been diagnosed as having Parkinson's Disease, which changed the situation completely. He felt unable to leave the family home now that both parents were ill:

> 'When I left school I was going to join up with the army, but my father got Parkinson's. I was going to join up for three years.' (Matt, age 19)

There may be a danger of young carers moving into caring jobs or professions because they feel these are the only skills they have to offer. Many of these jobs will be low paid with few prospects. However, while they may be lacking formal qualifications, the young people had many other qualities which employers would value, such as organisational skills, independence, maturity, etc. Currently these qualities are not validated or accredited in any way which employers would recognise.

Becoming an adult

When asked when they felt people become adults, many respondents suggested either a specific age – usually 16 or 18 – or a transitional phase such as leaving school, leaving home or becoming a parent. However, many also mentioned maturity, responsibility, decision-making and the acquisition of skills. These are the factors which many of the young people felt marked them out from their peers since they felt that they were more mature and responsible and had acquired a range of skills early in their lives. As we saw earlier, some of the respondents viewed this level of maturity and responsibility in a negative light while others saw it as a positive attribute.

Important factors mentioned were roles and situation, maturity, and transitions associated with a sudden change in circumstances:

'I suppose the general area would be about 18 but you can have what I think you could call "little adults", like what I felt I was at about 16, because I had the responsibility of what an adult person would have so, I kind of took on that role ... it's your situation and how you handle it and the responsibilities that you've got that make you what you are, an adult or whatever.' (Julie, age 21)

A young woman who left school at 15 to care for her father until he died said:

'Everyone's really different aren't they, they mature at different ages and stuff, between 16 and 20, 21 ... things I had to do with my dad I think I sort of become an adult when I were 15 in that way ... like a woman might be running a house, I were doing all the things maybe a 22 or 23-year-old would be doing. I think I become mature when I were 15.' (Sandra, age 19)

Another viewed himself as more mature than his older brother who had left the parental home early

and had not been involved in helping to support their father:

'Some people mature quicker than others. I know I've matured very quickly, I matured very early, yes. I wasn't really lucky for my teenage years, I had to look after my dad all the time, so I think I matured quite quickly. I know my brother, he's 17 and he's still childish ... basically it's just maturity isn't it. The more you mature the more you're classed as an adult.' (Ben, age 16)

Sometimes responsibility coincided with the sudden onset or exacerbation of parental illness:

'I think I became an adult overnight when that [stroke] happened to mam. I think it was just, I was thrown into being responsible then. I mean, obviously it will vary for different people and different situations. Some people my age haven't got a care in the world. I mean, my friend that used to live down the bottom of the street, she's got both parents at home. She's lived at home in the same house all her life. I've lived in about eight different places so far. And she still comes home with her laundry and things like that. ... I think being aware of other people's situations and appreciating, or even helping out with other people's situations can make you appreciate what you've got.' (Diana, age 23)

'I don't think there's a certain point, it just depends on your circumstances. I mean, I think I became an adult quite some time ago, when I was 16 because of the responsibilities, and I think it just depends on what responsibilities you take

up ... you could be 20-years-old and still your mum does everything for you.'
(Ravinder, age 19)

'I feel I became an adult when I was 15, when I had to live on my own and support myself [mother was in hospital for an extended period]. I think it's that or when you go out and get a job and you've got to, you know ... it's either when you have to go out to the real world and pay your own way, or when you've got to live on your own.' (Trish, age 16)

The most important transitional choices to be influenced by caring appear to be leaving home and choosing a career, possibly the two most important phases in becoming an adult. These decisions can be positively influenced, for example, a wish to help others or to use personal experience in a productive way in the labour market. In some cases, however, they can be restricted due to the absence of alternative support in the home – both informal and professional – and a lack of qualifications as a result of educational difficulties and missed schooling at an earlier age.

It is apparent from the responses that helping to care for and support a parent with an illness or disability can result in young people maturing more quickly than some of their peers. While some may have resented doing practical chores and taking responsibility when younger, as they grew older they realised the usefulness of these skills. The ability to care for oneself and others, to run a home and make decisions were often viewed in a positive light as young people began to make the transition to adulthood. Career choices can be positively influenced by caring, enabling young people to enter jobs and professions where their skills and past experiences will prove useful. More negative effects tend to be the result of educational problems and missed school earlier in life. Most respondents considered themselves to have reached or be approaching adulthood and their experiences as carers had often influenced this perception of themselves.

Summary of key findings

- Caring can have both positive and negative impacts on young people. Positive impacts: maturity, responsibility and life skills and a close and loving relationship with parents. Negative impacts: stress, depression, restricted social, educational and career opportunities, and less time for oneself.

- Young people's choices were both influenced and restricted by caring. The most important choices influenced appeared to be leaving home and choosing a career. Some young people left home either earlier or later than they would have chosen. Career and job choice were sometimes influenced by the skills gained through caring, but restricted by the lack of formal qualifications.

- Maturity, responsibility, decision-making and the acquisition of practical skills were seen as important for independence and adulthood. Young people often gained these from adopting a caring and supporting role within families. However, opportunity and other personal costs accompanied the acquisition of these skills. Providing support to an ill or disabled parent without appropriate family-centred services had immediate and long-term negative consequences for young people.

7 Conclusions and implications for policy and practice

The findings from the study indicate that children and young people who adopt inappropriate caring responsibilities can be affected not only during their childhood, but also as they make the transition from childhood to adulthood. It is the absence of family-focused, positive and supportive interventions by professionals, often combined with inadequate income, which cause the negative outcomes associated with caring by children and young people. The combination of family-centred support which enables disabled parents to parent their children effectively, coupled with specific support to children who require it, would do much to prevent children from adopting inappropriate roles and would prevent parents from having their independence undermined by having to accept this situation because of a lack of alternatives. The main factors that influence young people's caring experiences and transitions to adulthood are thus: service receipt, family income, the nature of parental illness or disability and family structure.

Young carers' transitions to adulthood can be influenced and affected in a variety of ways. While parental illness or disability can occasionally *directly* influence their children's transitions, it is usually an indirect influence. The most obvious direct influence is parent-child separation. This can happen as a result of parental death, hospitalisation or local authority care proceedings. Sometimes young people feel they can no longer remain with their parents *because* of their illness – this is usually where a parent has mental health problems.

The indirect influences and effects are many and varied, sometimes positive, more usually negative. A large proportion of respondents had missed school and gained no or minimal educational qualifications. This affected their transition from school into further/higher education and the labour market. Missing school was often linked to an absence of or inadequate service provision to ill or disabled parents, resulting in them often being left alone for long periods or having little support at times when help is most needed. Young people were sometimes reluctant to leave ill parents alone because they feared the consequences.

Almost all of the young people lived in families that were in receipt of welfare benefits. Many were living in poverty. None of the parents with illness or disability were in employment. Even previously affluent families may become poor if they rely on benefits for a prolonged period of time. Half of the respondents lived with lone parents. The combination of lone parenthood and illness or disability makes entire families vulnerable to poverty and social exclusion. The absence of a second adult in the home also resulted in children and young people within families taking on additional responsibilities. Where that lone parent had health problems, these responsibilities included the provision of care and support. Charging policies for social care services served to exacerbate poverty and resulted in some families cancelling services which were deemed too expensive or which were seen as poor value for money.

The emphasis on continuing education coupled with the lack of jobs for young people often exacerbated poverty. For those young people with caring responsibilities part-time work became difficult, sometimes impossible.

Caring can be stressful, particularly for young people living with parents who experience pain, mental distress, or who have a terminal or life-threatening illness. In a few cases stress and depression were severe enough to lead to physical and psychological ill health.

Helping to care for and support parents with ill

health sometimes results in maturity, self-reliance, independence and responsibility. The young people in the study exhibited a range of skills and competencies that aided transitions into adulthood. Many viewed the acquisition of these qualities and skills in a positive way. However, at the same time, many young carers were denied educational and employment opportunities because of their caring circumstances – a 'Catch 22' situation. The skills and competencies that they acquired therefore had opportunity costs, and providing care and support to family members in the absence of professional, external, acceptable support services cannot be considered as an acceptable way for young people to acquire these skills.

The study raises many implications for current and future policy in relation to children and young people, families and support for people with health and social care needs.

Policy and practice implications

- Many families received no or inadequate social care services. This resulted in children and young people sometimes adopting inappropriate roles. Even where services were provided they were sometimes inappropriate, intrusive or too costly. Service providers need to examine the level and types of services available and also the point at which these are offered. Early interventions may prevent inappropriate roles from becoming established.
- Services that support disabled adults in their parenting role are rare. While most local authorities now acknowledge the existence of young carers and mention them in community care or children and families service plans, the needs of disabled parents are rarely *specifically* mentioned.

- Professionals from all sectors need more understanding of the social model of disability.
- Social services, health, education and the voluntary sector all have a responsibility to prevent young caring from occurring by early recognition and positive interventions which focus on the needs of the whole family. If interventions are instigated early and are positive and supportive, then young caring should not become institutionalised within families nor be condoned by professionals.
- Assessments must recognise the needs and rights of both parents and children. Services must meet these needs and rights.
- Young people with caring responsibilities experience educational difficulties and disadvantages. Schools can compound these by not entering them for public examinations or by failing to recognise the specific educational, social and developmental needs of young carers.
- Those young carers who have negative educational experiences or who fare badly within the education system as a result of caring should be offered a 'second chance'. So too should those young people who terminate university studies as a result of having to care for a parent with ill health or disability.
- Where children and young people do miss school, there needs to be a better, more even balance between punitive interventions (such as threats of court action) and collusion (by condoning unauthorised absences).
- In some circumstances, particularly where a parent has a terminal illness, a balanced approach should meet the wishes of the child to spend time with their parent. Each case must be approached individually, but it is not acceptable to condone widespread school absences that can

seriously jeopardise young people's chances in later life.

- Many young carers often have key skills and competencies that go unrecognised and there is currently no way of accrediting such skills. While the acquisition of such skills will not be best achieved by caring unsupported, such skills, if acknowledged, would be an asset to many employers.

- Careers advisers need to be aware of these skills and competencies and try to offer a range of possible options rather than allowing young people to limit their choices to 'caring' jobs.

- The widespread absence of education maintenance allowances and grants for those in further and higher education discriminates against families where young people are unable to take part-time work because of caring commitments. Time-limited university grants and tuition fees discriminate against those students who fail to complete studies because of family problems, including parental illness, disability or death.

- There is a need to recognise and respond to the specific needs of young adult carers – those aged 18 to 25. There is little if any specialist provision for this group and these carers do not seem to make use of other (adult) carer support facilities while being too old to access most young carer provision.

- Children and young people have rights and some may choose to become carers for their parents. In such cases they should have the right to services and benefits which will assist them in their role as carers. Children and young people should not, however, feel obliged to care because of a lack of alternatives.

- The benefit system does not recognise the

particular needs of ill or disabled parents who have adolescent children. Assumptions are made regarding family or parental responsibilities to support their children for longer and longer periods of time. Poverty, illness, lone parenthood and lack of support may make this difficult.

- The lack of available single-person housing and age discrimination in relation to tenancies and leases can cause problems for early leavers who are, or feel, unable to remain in the parental home.

- Employment and education policies in particular need to be better coordinated to recognise the specific needs of young carers and the 'Catch 22' situations that many of them face. In some families caring might make financial sense in the absence of grants and awards; the skills and competencies young carers develop (which some identified as important for transitions) go largely unrecognised and unrewarded in the labour market; access to education and work is impaired as a result of caring.

- Health care professionals have a responsibility to ensure that adequate support and services are in place following illness or disability. More liaison between health and social care professionals and better provision and coordination of services will reduce families' reliance on children.

- While health care professionals have a duty and responsibility to provide families with information and advice relating to illness, disability, treatment, prognosis and care management, this should not extend to training children to perform inappropriate caring tasks.

- Currently some areas of the country have young carers projects while others do not. Some projects adopt a family focus and ameliorate the negative impacts of unsupported caring while others are less focussed. Disabled adults have little support as parents. Supporting either parent or child in isolation is not sufficient; support for whole families is essential.

A range of factors determines the quality and outcome of young carers' transitions to adulthood. While the nature of parental illness or disability, and family structure are important and inter-related influences, they only provide a partial explanation for young carers' experiences of vulnerability and transition. Other factors, external to families, have the major influence. The receipt, quality and timing of professional services and support, and the level and adequacy of family income, are critical. These interact with familial factors in complex ways, and in each family the various influences are likely to have different importance. But, in all cases, these are public issues, matters for professional practice and public policy, rather than merely private concerns.

Young carers' independence cannot be separated from their parent's independence. It is not possible to have true independence for one without independence for the other. Ill and disabled parents need to be supported as parents as well as disabled people, so that they can achieve personal independence and control over their own lives and provide the kind and quality of parenting to their children that they wish for. This will enable many families to prevent children from having to take on caring responsibilities in the first place, especially in the absence of any alternatives.

Young carers also need independence. They need to be able to make the best of their own lives, their childhood and the educational and other opportunities available to young people in a modern society. To secure these, the emphasis in policy and practice should be on preventing children from taking on inappropriate caring responsibilities in the first place, and stopping these roles from becoming institutionalised where and when they have already begun. Policies and services which identify and respond to the needs of all family members, but in particular those which support ill or disabled parents to enable them to prevent inappropriate caring roles from developing, will offer the best way forward. This challenges us all to think critically about how services to ill and disabled parents, and to existing young carers, should be structured, what they should do, and how they should fit together. Such a rethink would mean fundamental change to the existing structures for young carers services, and the emergence of new and empowering services for ill and disabled parents. Are we up to the challenge?

References

1   See Griffiths, Sir R. (1988) *Community Care: Agenda for Action*, London: HMSO; Department of Health (1989) *Caring for People: Community Care in the Next Decade and Beyond*, London: HMSO.

2   Becker, S. (2000) 'Young carers' in Davies, M. (Ed) *The Blackwell Encyclopaedia of Social Work*, London: Blackwell.

3   O'Neill, A. (1988) *Young Carers: The Tameside Research*, Tameside: Metropolitan Borough Council; Page, R. (1988) *Report on the Initial Survey Investigating the Number of Young Carers in Sandwell Secondary Schools*, Sandwell: Metropolitan Borough Council.

4   Bilsborrow, S. (1992) *'You Grow up Fast as Well … ' Young Carers on Merseyside*, Liverpool: Carers National Association, Personal Services Society and Barnardos.

5   Aldridge, J. and Becker, S. (1993) *Children Who Care: Inside the World of Young Carers*, Loughborough: Young Carers Research Group, Loughborough University.

6   Aldridge, J. and Becker, S. (1994) *My Child, My Carer: The Parents' Perspective*, Loughborough: Young Carers Research Group, Loughborough University.

7   Grimshaw, R. (1991) *Children of Parents with Parkinson's Disease: A Research Report for the Parkinson's Disease Society*, London: National Children's Bureau.

8   Elliott, A. (1992) *Hidden Children: A Study of Ex-Young Carers of Parents with Mental Health Problems in Leeds*, Leeds: City Council, Mental Health Development Section; Landells, S. and Pritlove, J. (1994) *Young Carers of a Parent with Schizophrenia: A Leeds Survey*, Leeds: City Council, Department of Social Services.

9   Segal, J. and Simkins, J. (1993) *My Mum Needs Me: Helping Children with Ill or Disabled Parents*, Harmondsworth: Penguin; Segal, J. and Simkins, J. (1996) *Helping Children with Ill or Disabled Parents: A Guide for Parents and Professionals*, London: Jessica Kingsley.

10 Imrie, J. and Coombes, Y. (1995) *No Time to Waste: The Scale and Dimensions of the Problem of Children Affected by HIV/AIDS in the United Kingdom*, Ilford: Barnardos.

11 Dearden, C. and Becker, S. (1995) *Young Carers: The Facts*, Sutton: Reed Business Publishing.

12 Dearden, C. and Becker, S. (1998) *Young Carers in the United Kingdom: A Profile*, London: Carers National Association.

13 See for example Department of Health (1996a) *Carers (Recognition and Services) Act 1995: Policy Guidance and Practice Guide*, London: Department of Health; Department of Health (1999) *Caring About Carers: A National Strategy for Carers*, London: Department of Health.

14 Department of Health (1996b) *Young Carers: Making a Start*, London: Department of Health; Department of Health (1996c) *Young Carers: Something to Think About*, London: Department of Health.

15 Walker, A. (1996) *Young Carers and their Families*, London: The Stationery Office.

16 Becker (2000) op. cit.

17 Keith, L. and Morris, J. (1995) 'Easy targets: a disability rights perspective on the "children as carers" debate', *Critical Social Policy*, 44/45: 36–57.

18 Parker, G. and Olsen, R. (1995) 'A sideways glance at young carers' in Department of Health *Young Carers: Something to Think About. Papers Presented at Four SSI Workshops May – July 1995*, London: Department of Health.

19 Department of Health (1998) *Quality Protects: Framework for Action*, London: The Stationery Office.

20 Dearden and Becker (1998) op. cit.

21 See Department of Health (2000) *Framework for the Assessment of Children in Need and their Families*, London: Departmen of Health; Department of Health (2000) *The Child's World: Assessing Children in Need*, London: Department of Health, NSPCC and University of Sheffield.

22 Barnardos' Policy Development Unit (1996) *Transition to Adulthood*, Ilford: Barnardos, p.9.

23 Dearden and Becker (1995) and (1998) op. cit.

24 Shah, R. and Hatton, C. (1999) *Caring Alone: Young Carers in South Asian Communities*, Ilford: Barnardos.

25 Lindlof, T.R. (1995) *Qualitative Communication Research Methods*, Thousand Oaks, California: Sage.

26 Glaser, B.G. and Strauss, A.L. (1967) T*he Discovery of Grounded Theory*, Chicago: Aldine.

27 Aldridge and Becker (1994) op. cit.

28 See Becker, S., Aldridge, J. and Dearden, C. (1998) *Young Carers and Their Families*, Oxford: Blackwell Science; Dearden and Becker (1998) op. cit.

29 See for example Black, Sir D. (1980) *Inequalities in Health: Report of a Research Working Group*, London: DHSS; Barnes, C. (1992) 'Discrimination, disability benefits and the 1980s', *Benefits*, 3: 3–7.

30 Dearden and Becker, (1995) and (1998) op. cit.

31 Ibid.

32 Dearden and Becker (1998) op. cit.

33 Barnardos (1996) op. cit. p. 27.

34 See for example Aldridge and Becker (1993) op. cit.; Fox, N.J. (1995) 'Professional models of school absence associated with home responsibility', *British Journal of Sociology of Education*, 16: 2: 221–42; Marsden, R. (1995) *Young Carers and Education*, London: Borough of Enfield Education Department.

35 Dearden and Becker, (1995) op. cit.

36 Dearden and Becker, (1998) op. cit.

37 Department for Education and Employment (1999) *Tackling Truancy Together*, London: DfEE.

38 Roll, J. (1990) *Young People: Growing up in the Welfare State*, London: Family Policy Studies Centre.

39 Barnardos (1996) op. cit.

40 Hollands, R.G. (1990) *The Long Transition: Class, Culture and Youth Training*, Basingstoke: Macmillan.

41 Irwin, S. (1995) *Rights of Passage: Social Change and the Transition from Youth to Adulthood*, London: UCL Press.

42 Jones, G. and Wallace, C. (1992) *Youth, Family and Citizenship*, Buckingham: Open University Press, p. 24.

43 Irwin (1995) op. cit. p. 65.

44 Black, (1980) op. cit.; Barnes, (1992) op.cit.

45 Jones and Wallace (1992) op.cit.

46 Ibid.

47 Series of reports produced by SSI during 1999 and 2000 under the umbrella title *Inspection of Services to Support Disabled Adults in Their Parenting Role*, London: Department of Health.

48 Employment Options, Inc. (1997) *Moving Towards our Vision: Annual Report 1996–97*, Marlboro: Massachusetts.

49 Department of Health (1998) *Children Looked After by Local Authorities Year Ending 31 March 1997*, London: Department of Health.